Kubernetes
The Complete Guide
To Master Kubernetes
(March 2019 Edition)

COPYRIGHT 2019 by Joseph D. Moore

Copyright

In no way is it legal to reproduce, duplicate, or transmit any part of this document in either electronic means or in printed format. Recording of this publication is strictly prohibited and any storage of this document is not allowed unless with written permission from the publisher. All rights reserved.

The information provided herein is stated to be truthful and consistent, in that any liability, in terms of inattention or otherwise, by any usage or abuse of any policies, processes, or directions contained within is the solitary and utter responsibility of the recipient reader. Under no circumstances will any legal responsibility or blame be held against the publisher for any reparation, damages, or monetary loss due to the information herein, either directly or indirectly.

Respective authors own all copyrights not held by the publisher. The information herein is offered for informational purposes solely, and is universal as so. The presentation of the information is without contract or any type of guarantee assurance.

The trademarks that are used are without any consent, and the publication of the trademark is without permission or backing by the trademark owner. All trademarks and brands within this book are for clarifying purposes only and are the owned by the owners themselves, not affiliated with this document.

TABLE OF CONTENTS

INTRODUCTION 5
WHAT IS KUBERNETES? 8
WHAT IS KUBERNETES NETWORKING? 15
INTRODUCTION TO KUBERNETES MONITORING 21
KUBERNETES MONITORING 29
TOP OPEN-SOURCE TOOLS FOR MONITORING KUBERNETES 35
KUBERNETES MONITORING: BEST PRACTICES, METHODS, AND EXISTING
    SOLUTIONS 40
THE STATE OF KUBERNETES CONFIGURATION MANAGEMENT: AN
    UNSOLVED PROBLEM 48
AN INTRODUCTION TO HELM, THE PACKAGE MANAGER FOR
    KUBERNETES 60
KUBERNETES HELM 67
HOW TO CREATE A KUBERNETES CLUSTER USING KUBEADM 72
DEPLOY, SCALE AND UPGRADE AN APPLICATION ON KUBERNETES WITH
    HELM 86
KUBERNETES DEPLOYMENT 93
KUBERNETES SERVICES 100
KUBERNETES ON AWS 108
BENEFITS OF KUBERNETES 126

THE BENEFITS AND BUSINESS VALUE OF KUBERNETES 133
HOW TO DEVELOP KUBERNETES-FRIENDLY CONTAINERISED
    APPLICATIONS 144
WHAT IS THE DIFFERENCE BETWEEN KUBERNETES AND DOCKER? 179
THE ADVANTAGES OF USING KUBERNETES AND DOCKER TOGETHER 183
KUBERNETES VS DOCKER SWARM 194
DOCKER VS. KUBERNETES VS. APACHE MESOS: WHY WHAT YOU THINK
    YOU KNOW IS PROBABLY WRONG 199
WHAT IS CLOUD-NATIVE? 209
MICROSERVICES VERSUS APIS 216
WHAT IS MICROSERVICES? 224

INTRODUCTION

Emerging cloud computing technologies have evolved more with the open source. New ideas are now becoming technological solutions for enterprises with increasing demands for complex and highly scalable technologies. The advanced cloud ecosystem has become more efficient for both development and IT operations teams of start-ups as well as established enterprises.

Introducing Kubernetes - Technical Overview:

For automated deployment, scaling, monitoring and operations of application cloud containers, it is the most efficient open-source platform. It includes all essential elements with greater scalability options as a complete container-centric infrastructure. Since automation remains the core part of this, professional resource optimizations, adding new features for the end users by scaling up the resources have become more obvious with this option.

Integration through Cloud Containers:

There are many reasons why the enterprises are switching to cloud platforms and containers. To get rid of heavyweight and non-portable architecture; deployment of small, fast yet portable technology platforms are getting the best impact. Instead of hardware virtualizations, the newest way of deploying applications through containers focusing on operating-system-level virtualization. In this way, we can put an end to the limitations of the host through choosing executable file-systems, libraries, and etc.

Adding the most advanced feature of automation of workflow and workload balancing can be simplified with Kubernetes. Scheduling and running application containers along with developing a container-centric development environment is possible with it. Whether on physical or virtual machines, it can be utilized on all platforms with ease.

Installing and Accessing the Cluster:

Setup or installation of the system varies according to the host OS, through different modules. Kubeadm is used for installations on Linux, kops for AWS, are the most common options available. Similarly, for accessing the clusters and sharing it through kubeconfig is much easier. Kubeconfig also adds security features to authenticate every access to the clusters.

Its web-based User-Interface or Web UI includes all controls. This dashboard can be accessed remotely for setting up, controlling and monitoring the processes of containers on the clusters. The online user guide and the community that supports this technology are much active to help in installations of the system.

The Ease of Deployment:

With the simplified configuring modules, launching or deploying applications on cloud containers happens on the go. Well management of resources and replication controller has become an essential part of workload deployment and management segment. Performing batch jobs on this cloud environment and the processes of corn jobs can be resourcefully done here.

With Kubernetes, connecting applications with appropriate services through configuring firewalls of the cloud service providers can be done at once. In complex configurations, creating an external load balancer and use of federated services to discover cross-cluster service. Resource usage monitoring, process logging and like jobs become more accessible with specified modules available on the dashboard. Administrating clusters, installing add-ons, rolling out new features and updates have become more resourceful on a cloud container environment. Configuring or connecting this automated workflow system on other advanced aspects makes the processes more resourceful.

WHAT IS KUBERNETES?

Kubernetes is an open source orchestration tool developed by Google for managing microservices or containerized applications across a distributed cluster of nodes. Kubernetes provides highly resilient infrastructure with zero downtime readying capabilities, automatic rollback, scaling, and self-healing of containers (which consists of auto-placement, auto-restart, auto-replication , and scaling of containers on the basis of hardware usage).

The main objective of Kubernetes is to hide the complexity of managing a fleet of containers by providing REST arthropod genus for the needed functionalities. Kubernetes is portable in nature, meaning it can run on numerous public or private cloud platforms such as AWS, Azure, OpenStack, or Apache Mesos. It will also run on vacant metal machines.

Kubernetes Components and Architecture

Kubernetes follows a client-server architecture. It's possible to have a multi-master setup (for high availability), but by default there is a single master server which acts as a controlling node and point of contact. The master server consists of various components including a kube-apiserver, an etcd storage, a kube-controller-manager, a cloud-controller-manager, a kube-scheduler, and a DNS server for Kubernetes services. Node components include kubelet and kube-proxy on top of Docker.

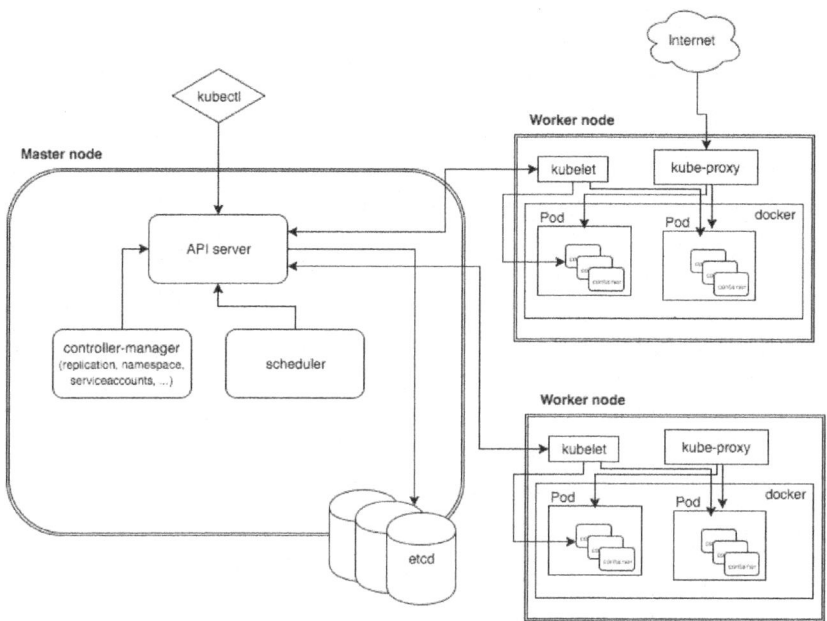

Master Components

Below are the main components found on the master node:

- etcd cluster - a simple, distributed key value storage which is used to store the Kubernetes cluster data (such as number of pods, their state, namespace, etc), API objects and service discovery details. It is only accessible from the API server for security reasons. etcd enables notifications to the cluster about configuration changes with the help of watchers. Notifications are API requests on each etcd cluster node to trigger the update of information in the node's storage.
- kube-apiserver - Kubernetes API server is the central management entity that receives all REST requests for modifications (to pods, services, replication sets/controllers and others), serving as

frontend to the cluster. Also, this is the only component that communicates with the etcd cluster, making sure data is stored in etcd and is in agreement with the service details of the deployed pods.
- kube-controller-manager - runs a number of distinct controller processes in the background (for example, replication controller controls number of replicas in a pod, endpoints controller populates endpoint objects like services and pods, and others) to regulate the shared state of the cluster and perform routine tasks. When a change in a service configuration occurs (for example, replacing the image from which the pods are running, or changing parameters in the configuration yaml file), the controller spots the change and starts working towards the new desired state.
- cloud-controller-manager - is responsible for managing controller processes with dependencies on the underlying cloud provider (if applicable). For example, when a controller needs to check if a node was terminated or set up routes, load balancers or volumes in the cloud infrastructure, all that is handled by the cloud-controller-manager.
- kube-scheduler - helps schedule the pods (a co-located group of containers inside which our application processes are running) on the various nodes based on resource utilization. It reads the service's operational requirements and schedules it on the best fit node. For example, if the application needs 1GB of memory and 2 CPU cores, then the pods for that application will be scheduled on a node with at least those resources. The scheduler runs each time there is a need to schedule pods. The scheduler must know the total resources available as well as resources allocated to existing workloads on each node.

Node (worker) components

Below are the main components found on a (worker) node:

- kubelet - the main service on a node, regularly taking in new or modified pod specifications (primarily through the kube-apiserver) and ensuring that pods and their containers are healthy and running in the desired state. This component also reports to the master on the health of the host where it is running.
- kube-proxy - a proxy service that runs on each worker node to deal with individual host subnetting and expose services to the external world. It performs request forwarding to the correct pods/containers across the various isolated networks in a cluster.

Kubectl

kubectl command is a line tool that interacts with kube-apiserver and send commands to the master node. Each command is converted into an API call.

Kubernetes Concepts

Making use of Kubernetes requires understanding the different abstractions it uses to represent the state of the system, such as services, pods, volumes, namespaces, and deployments.
- Pod - generally refers to one or more containers that should be controlled as a single application. A pod encapsulates application containers, storage resources, a unique network ID and other configuration on how to run the containers.

- Service - pods are volatile, that is Kubernetes does not guarantee a given physical pod will be kept alive (for instance, the replication controller might kill and start a new set of pods). Instead, a service represents a logical set of pods and acts as a gateway, allowing (client) pods to send requests to the service without needing to keep track of which physical pods actually make up the service.
- Volume - similar to a container volume in Docker, but a Kubernetes volume applies to a whole pod and is mounted on all containers in the pod. Kubernetes guarantees data is preserved across container restarts. The volume will be removed only when the pod gets destroyed. Also, a pod can have multiple volumes (possibly of different types) associated.
- Namespace - a virtual cluster (a single physical cluster can run multiple virtual ones) intended for environments with many users spread across multiple teams or projects, for isolation of concerns. Resources inside a namespace must be unique and cannot access resources in a different namespace. Also, a namespace can be allocated a resource quota to avoid consuming more than its share of the physical cluster's overall resources.
- Deployment - describes the desired state of a pod or a replica set, in a yaml file. The deployment controller then gradually updates the environment (for example, creating or deleting replicas) until the current state matches the desired state specified in the deployment file. For example, if the yaml file defines 2 replicas for a pod but only one is currently running, an extra one will get created. Note that replicas managed via a deployment should not be manipulated directly, only via new deployments.

Kubernetes Design Principles

Kubernetes was designed to support the features required by highly available distributed systems, such as (auto-)scaling, high availability, security and portability.

- Scalability - Kubernetes provides horizontal scaling of pods on the basis of CPU utilization. The threshold for CPU usage is configurable and Kubernetes will automatically start new pods if the threshold is reached. For example, if the threshold is 70% for CPU but the application is actually growing up to 220%, then eventually 3 more pods will be deployed so that the average CPU utilization is back under 70%. When there are multiple pods for a particular application, Kubernetes provides the load balancing capacity across them. Kubernetes also supports horizontal scaling of stateful pods, including NoSQL and RDBMS databases through Stateful sets. A Stateful set is a similar concept to a Deployment, but ensures storage is persistent and stable, even when a pod is removed.
- High Availability - Kubernetes addresses highly availability both at application and infrastructure level. Replica sets ensure that the desired (minimum) number of replicas of a stateless pod for a given application are running. Stateful sets perform the same role for stateful pods. At the infrastructure level, Kubernetes supports various distributed storage backends like AWS EBS, Azure Disk, Google Persistent Disk, NFS, and more. Adding a reliable, available storage layer to Kubernetes ensures high availability of stateful workloads. Also, each of the master components can be configured for multi-node replication (multi-master) to ensure

higher availability.

- Security - Kubernetes addresses security at multiple levels: cluster, application and network. The API endpoints are secured through transport layer security (TLS). Only authenticated users (either service accounts or regular users) can execute operations on the cluster (via API requests). At the application level, Kubernetes secrets can store sensitive information (such as passwords or tokens) per cluster (a virtual cluster if using namespaces, physical otherwise). Note that secrets are accessible from any pod in the same cluster. Network policies for access to pods can be defined in a deployment. A network policy specifies how pods are allowed to communicate with each other and with other network endpoints.
- Portability - Kubernetes portability manifests in terms of operating system choices (a cluster can run on any mainstream Linux distribution), processor architectures (either virtual machines or bare metal), cloud providers (AWS, Azure or Google Cloud Platform), and new container runtimes, besides Docker, can also be added. Through the concept of federation, it can also support workloads across hybrid (private and public cloud) or multi-cloud environments. This also supports availability zone fault tolerance within a single cloud provider.

WHAT IS KUBERNETES NETWORKING?

Since a Kubernetes cluster consists of various nodes and pods, understanding how they communicate between them is essential. The Kubernetes networking model supports different types of open source implementations. Kubernetes provides an IP address to each pod so that there is no need to map host ports to container ports as in the Docker networking model. Pods behave much like VMs or physical hosts with respect to port allocation, naming, load balancing and application configuration. For more background on Kubernetes components, see Kuberenetes Architecture.

Kubernetes vs. Docker Networking Model

The Docker networking model relies, by default, on a virtual bridge network called Docker0. It is a per-host private network where containers get attached (and thus can reach each other) and allocated a private IP address. This means containers running on different machines are not able to communicate with each other (as they are attached to different hosts' networks). In order to communicate across nodes with Docker, we have to map host ports to container ports and proxy the traffic. In this scenario, it's up to the Docker operator to avoid port clashes between containers.

The Kubernetes networking model, on the other hand, natively supports multi-host networking in which pods are able to communicate with each other by default, regardless of which host they live in. Kubernetes does not provide an implementation of this model by default, rather it relies on third-party tools that comply with the following requirements: all containers are able to communicate with each other without NAT; nodes are able to communicate with containers without NAT; and a container's IP address is the same from inside and outside the container.

Kubernetes follows an "IP-per-pod" model where each pod get assigned an IP address and all containers in a single pod share the same network namespaces and IP address. Containers in the same pod can therefore reach each other's ports via localhost:<port>. However, it is not recommended to communicate directly with a pod via its IP address due to pod's volatility (a pod can be killed and replaced at any moment). Instead, use a Kubernetes service which represents a group of pods acting as a single entity to the outside. Services get allocated their own IP address in the cluster and provide a reliable entry point.

Kubernetes Networking Model Implementations

Kubernetes does not provide a default network implementation, it only enforces a model for third-party tools to implement. There is a variety of implementations nowadays, below we list some popular ones.

- Flannel - a very simple overlay network that satisfies the Kubernetes requirements. Flannel runs an agent on each host and allocates a subnet lease to each of them out of a larger, preconfigured address space.
- Flannel creates a flat network called as overlay network which runs above the host network.
- Project Calico - an open source container networking provider and network policy engine. Calico provides a highly scalable

networking and network policy solution for connecting Kubernetes pods based on the same IP networking principles as the internet. Calico can be deployed without encapsulation or overlays to provide high-performance, high-scale data center networking.
- Weave Net - a cloud native networking toolkit which provides a resilient and simple to use (does not require any configuration) network for Kubernetes and its hosted applications. It provides various functionalities like scaling, service discovery, performance without complexity and secure networking.

Other options include Cisco ACI , Cilium , Contiv , Contrail , Kube-router , Nuage , OVN , Romana , VMWare NSX-T with NSX-T Container Plug-in (NCP) . Some tools even support using multiple implementations, such as Huawei CNI-Genie and Multus .

How Pods Communicate with Each Other

Because each pod has a unique IP in a flat address space inside the Kubernetes cluster, direct pod-to-pod communication is possible without requiring any kind of proxy or address translation. This also allows using standard ports for most applications as there is no need to route traffic from a host port to a container port, as in Docker. Note that because all containers in a pod share the same IP address, container-private ports are not possible (containers can access each other's ports **via localhost:<port>**) and port conflicts are possible. However, the typical use case for a pod is to run a single application service (in a similar fashion to a VM), in which case port conflicts are a rare situation.

How Pods Communicate with Services

Kubernetes services allow grouping pods under a common access policy (for example, load-balanced). The service gets assigned a virtual IP which pods outside the service can communicate with. Those requests are then transparently proxied (via the kube-proxy component that runs on each node) to the pods inside the service. Different proxy-modes are supported:

- iptables : kube-proxy installs iptables rules trap access to service IP addresses and redirect them to the correct pods.

- userspace : kube-proxy opens a port (randomly chosen) on the local node. Requests on this "proxy port" get proxied to one of the service's pods (as retrieved from Endpoints API).

- ipvs (from Kubernetes 1.9): calls netlink interface to create ipvs rules and regularly synchronizes them with the Endpoints API.

Kubernetes also offers an Endpoints API for Kubernetes native applications that is updated whenever the set of pods in a service changes. This allows a pod to retrieve the current endpoints for all pods in a service.

Incoming Traffic from the Outside World

Nodes inside a Kubernetes cluster are firewalled from the Internet by default, thus services IP addresses are only targetable within the cluster network. In order to allow incoming traffic from outside the cluster, a service specification can map the service to one or more externalIPs (external to the cluster). Requests arriving at an external IP address get routed by the underlying cloud provider to a node in the cluster (usually via a load balancer outside Kubernetes). The node then knows which service is mapped to the external IP and also which pods are part of the service, thus routing the request to an appropriate pod.

To support more complex policies on incoming traffic, Kubernetes provides an Ingress API offering externally-reachable URLs, traffic load balancing, SSL termination, and name based virtual hosting to services. An ingress is a collection of rules that allow inbound connections to reach the cluster service. Note that to actually action ingresses specified via the API, an ingress controller (such as the NGINX ingress controller) must be deployed and configured for the cluster. This might be done automatically or not, depending on which Kubernetes cloud provider you are using.

DNS for Services and Pods

Kubernetes provides its own DNS service to resolve domain names inside the cluster in order for pods to communicate with each other. This is implemented by deploying a regular Kubernetes service which does name resolution inside the cluster, and configuring individual containers to contact the DNS service to resolve domain names. Note that this "internal DNS" is compatible and expected to run along with the cloud provider's DNS service.

Every service gets assigned a DNS name which resolves to the cluster IP of the service. The naming convention includes the service name and its namespace. For example:

my-service.my-namespace.svc.cluster.local

A pod inside the same namespace as the service does not need to fully qualify its name, for example a pod in my-namespace could lookup this service with a DNS query for my-service , while a pod outside my-namespace would have to query for my-service.my-namespace .

For headless services (without a cluster IP), the DNS name resolves to the set of IPs of the pods which are part of the service. The caller can then use the set of IPs as it sees fit (for example round-robin).

By default pods get assigned a DNS name which includes the pod's IP address and namespace. In order to assign a more meaningful DNS name, the pod's specification can specify a hostname and subdomain:

Network Extensions

Network extensions are the way to extend or enhance the networking by introducing various network functionalities such as cross-node networking or network policies. There are two types of network extensions or plugins:

- CNI plugin: designed for interoperability, this plugin implements the Container Network Interface (CNI) specification inserting a network interface into the container network namespace (e.g. one end of a veth pair) and making any necessary changes on the host (for example, attaching the other end of the veth into a bridge).
- Kubenet plugin : a simple plugin for Linux usage only, typically used together with a cloud provider that sets up routing rules for communication between nodes.

INTRODUCTION TO KUBERNETES MONITORING

Introduction

With over 40,000 stars on Github, more than 70,000 commits, and with major contributors like Google and Redhat, Kubernetes has rapidly taken over the container ecosystem to become the true leader of container orchestration platforms.
Understanding Kubernetes and Its Abstractions

At the infrastructure level, a Kubernetes cluster is a set of physical or virtual machines acting in a specific role. The machines acting in the role of Master act as the brain of all operations and are charged with orchestrating containers that run on all of the Nodes.

Master components manage the lifecycle of a pod, the base unit of deployment within a Kubernetes cluster. If a pod dies, the Controller creates a new one. If you scale the number of pod replicas up or down, the Controller creates or destroys pods to satisfy your request. The Master role includes the following components:

- kube-apiserver - exposes APIs for the other master components.
- etcd - a consistent and highly-available key/value store used for storing all internal cluster data.
- kube-scheduler - uses information in the Pod spec to decide on which Node to run a Pod.

- kube-controller-manager - responsible for Node management (detecting if a Node fails), pod replication, and endpoint creation.
- cloud-controller-manager - runs controllers that interact with the underlying cloud providers.

Node components are worker machines in Kubernetes and are managed by the Master. A node may be a virtual machine (VM) or physical machine, and Kubernetes runs equally well on both types of systems. Each node contains the necessary components to run pods:
- kubelet: handles all communication between the Master and the node on which it is running. It interfaces with the container runtime to deploy and monitor containers.
- kube-proxy: maintains the network rules on the host and handles transmission of packets between pods, the host, and the outside world.
- container runtime: responsible for running containers on the host. The most popular engine is Docker, although Kubernetes supports container runtimes from rkt, runc and others.

From a logical perspective, a Kubernetes deployment is comprised of various components, each serving a specific purpose within the cluster.

- Pods are the basic unit of deployment within Kubernetes. A pod consists of one or more containers that share the same network namespace and IP address. Best practices recommend that you create one pod per application component so you can scale and control them separately.

- Services provide a consistent IP address in front of a set of pods and a policy that controls access to them. The set of pods targeted by a service is often determined by a label selector. This makes it easy to point the service to a different set of pods during upgrades or blue/green deployments.

- ReplicaSets are controlled by deployments and ensure that the desired number of pods for that deployment are running.

- Namespaces define a logical namespace for resources such as pods and services. They enable resources to use the same names, whereas resources in a single namespace must have unique names. Rancher uses namespaces with its role-based access control to provide a secure separation between namespaces and the resources running inside of them.

- Metadata marks containers based on their deployment characteristics.

Monitoring Kubernetes

Multiple services and namespaces can be spread across the infrastructure. As seen above, each of the services are made of pods, which can have one or more containers inside. With so many moving parts, monitoring even a small Kubernetes cluster can present a challenge. It requires a deep understanding of the application architecture and functionality in order to monitor it effectively.

Kubernetes ships with tools for monitoring the cluster:

   Probes actively monitor the health of a container. If the probe determines that a container is no longer healthy, the probe will restart it.

   cAdvisor is an open source agent that monitors resource usage and analyzes the performance of containers. Originally created by Google, cAdvisor is now integrated with the Kubelet. It collects, aggregates, processes and exports metrics such as CPU, memory, file and network usage for all containers running on a given node.

   The kubernetes dashboard is an add-on which gives an overview of the resources running on your cluster. It also gives a very basic means of deploying and interacting with those resources.

Kubernetes has tremendous capability for automatically recovering from failures. It can restart pods if a process crashes, and it will redistribute pods if a node fails. However, for all of its power, there are times when it cannot fix a problem. In order to detect those situations, we need additional monitoring.

Layers Of Monitoring

Infrastructure

All clusters should have monitoring of the underlying server components because problems at the server level will show up in the workloads.

What to monitor?

- CPU utilization. Monitoring the CPU will reveal both system and user consumption, and it will also show iowait. When running clusters in the cloud or with any network storage, iowait will indicate bottlenecks waiting for storage reads and writes (i/o processes). An oversubscribed storage framework can impact performance.

- Memory usage. Monitoring memory will show how much memory is in use and how much is available, either as free memory or as cache. Systems that run up against memory limits will begin to swap (if swap is available on the system), and swapping will rapidly degrade performance.

- Disk pressure. If a system is running write-intensive services like etcd or any datastore, running out of disk space can be catastrophic. The inability to write data will result in corruption, and that corruption can transfer to real-world losses. Technologies like LVM make it trivial to grow disk space as needed, but keeping an eye on it is imperative.

- Network bandwidth. In today's era of gigabit interfaces, it might seem like you can never run out of bandwidth. However, it doesn't take more than a few aberrant services, a data breach, system compromise, or DOS attack to eat up all of the bandwidth and cause an outage. Keeping awareness of your normal data consumption and the patterns of your application will help you keep costs down and also aid in capacity planning.

- Pod resources. The Kubernetes scheduler works best when it knows what resources a pod needs. It can then assure that it places pods on nodes where the resources are available. When designing your network, consider how many nodes can fail before the remaining nodes can no longer run all of the desired resources. Using a service such as a cloud autoscaling group will make recovery quick, but be sure that the remaining nodes can handle the increased load for the time that it takes to bring the failed node back online.

Kubernetes Services

All of the components that make up a Kubernetes Master or Worker, including etcd, are critical to the health of your applications. If any of these fail, the monitoring system needs to detect the failure and either fix it or send an alert.

Internal Services

The final layer is that of the Kubernetes resources themselves. Kubernetes exposes metrics about the resources, and we can also monitor the applications directly. Although we can trust that Kubernetes will work to maintain the desired state, if it's unable to do so, we need a way for a human to intervene and fix the issue.

Monitoring with Rancher

In addition to managing Kubernetes clusters running anywhere, on any provider, Rancher will also monitor the resources running inside of those clusters and send alerts when they exceed defined thresholds.

There are already dozens of tutorials on how to deploy Rancher. If you don't already have a cluster running, pause here and visit our quickstart guide to spin one up. When it's running, return here to continue with monitoring.

The cluster overview gives you an idea of the resources in use and the state of the Kubernetes components. In our case, we're using 78% of the CPU, 26% of the RAM and 11% of the maximum number of pods we can run within the cluster.

When you select the name of the workload, Rancher presents a page that shows information about it. At the top of this page it will show you each of the pods, which node they're on, their IP address, and their state. Clicking on any individual pod takes us one level deeper, where now we see detailed information about only that pod. The hamburger menu icon in the top right corner lets us interact with the pod, and through this we can execute a shell, view the logs, or delete the pod.

Use Prometheus for Monitoring

The information visible in the Rancher UI is useful for troubleshooting, but it's not the best way to actively track the state of the cluster throughout every moment of its life. For that we'll use Prometheus, a sibling project of Kubernetes under the care and guidance of the Cloud Native Computing Foundation. We'll also use Grafana, a tool for converting time-series data into beautiful graphs and dashboards.

Prometheus is an open-source application for monitoring systems and generating alerts. It can monitor almost anything, from servers to applications, databases, or even a single process. In the Prometheus lexicon it monitors targets, and each unit of a target is called a metric. The act of retrieving information about a target is known as scraping. Prometheus will scrape targets at designated intervals and store the information in a time-series database. Prometheus has its own scripting language called PromQL.

Grafana is also open source and runs as a web application. Although frequently used with Prometheus, it also supports backend datastores such as InfluxDB, Graphite, Elasticsearch, and others. Grafana makes it easy to create graphs and assemble those graphs into dashboards. Those dashboards can be protected by a strong authentication and authorization layer, and they can also be shared with others without giving them access to the server itself. Grafana makes heavy use of JSON for its object definitions, which makes its graphs and dashboards extremely portable and easy to use with version control.

In conclusion

Kubernetes works tirelessly to keep your applications running, but that doesn't free you from the obligation of staying aware of how they're doing. As soon as you begin to rely on Kubernetes to do work for you, the responsible thing to do is deploy a monitoring system that keeps you informed and empowers you to make decisions.

Prometheus and Grafana will do this for you, and when you use Rancher, the time it would normally take to deploy these two applications is reduced to mere minutes.

KUBERNETES MONITORING

Understanding Kubernetes monitoring pipeline(s) is essential to help you diagnose run-time problems and to manage the scale of your pods, and cluster. Monitoring is one of these areas that are evolving very rapidly inside Kubernetes. It has a lot of pieces that are still in the influx and hence some confusion. My goal as I hope in this chapter is to clarify it a bit and to give you a good starting point.

Kubernetes has two monitoring pipelines: (1) The core metrics pipeline, which is an integral part of Kubernetes and always installed with all distributions, and (2) The services monitoring (non-core) pipeline, which is a separate pipeline, and Kubernetes has no or limited dependency on. Keep reading to learn why :)

Core Monitoring Pipeline

Sometimes is referred to as the resource metrics pipeline. The core monitoring pipeline is installed with every distribution. It provides enough details to other components inside the Kubernetes cluster to run as expected, such as the scheduler to allocate pods and containers, HPA and VPA to take proper decisions scaling pods.

The way it works is relatively simple:

- CAdvisor collects metrics about containers and nodes that on which it is installed. Note: CAdvisor is installed by default on all cluster nodes

- Kubelet exposes these metrics (default is one-minute resolution) through Kubelet APIs.
- Metrics Server discovers all available nodes and calls Kubelet API to get containers and nodes resources usage.
- Metrics Server exposes these metrics through Kubernetes aggregation API.

A few helpful points

- Kubelet cannot run without CAdvisor. If you try to uninstall it or stop it, the cluster's behavior will become unpredictable.
- Even though Heapster "soon to be deprecated" is currently dependent on CAdvisor, but CAdvisor is not going away anytime soon.

Services Monitoring Pipeline

Services pipeline in abstract terms is relatively simple. Confusion usually comes from the plethora of services, agents that you can mix and match to get your pipeline up and running. Also, you can blame Heapster for that :)

Services Monitoring Pipeline consists of three main components: (1) Collection agent, (2) Metrics Server, and (3) Dashboards. I'll not talk about alerting because it has lots of interesting twists :)

Below is the typical workflow, including most common components

- Monitoring agent collects node metrics. cAdvisor collects containers and pods metrics.

- Monitoring Aggregation service collects data from its own agent and cAdvisor.
- Data is stored in the monitoring system's storage.
- Monitoring aggregation service exposes metrics through APIs and dashboards.

A Few Notes:

- Prometheus is the official monitoring server sponsored and incubated by CNCF. It integrates directly with cAdvisor. You don't need to install a 3rd party agent to retrieve additional metrics about your containers. However, if you need deeper insights about each node, you need to install an agent of your choice — see Prometheus integrations and third-party exporters page.
- Almost all monitoring systems piggyback on Kubernetes scheduling and orchestration. For example, their agents are installed as DeomonSets and depend on Kubernetes scheduler to have an instance scheduled on each node.
- Most monitoring agents depend on Kubelet to collect container relevant metrics, which in turn depends on cAdvisor. Very few agents collect container relevant details independently.
- Most monitoring aggregation services depend on agents pushing metrics to them. Prometheus is an exception. It pulls metrics out of the installed agents.

What should you consider in Kubernetes Services Pipeline?

Ideal Services pipeline depends on two main factors: (1) collection of relevant metrics, (2) Awareness of continuous changes inside kubernetes cluster.

A good pipeline should focus on collecting relevant metrics. There are plenty of agents that can collect OS and process-level metrics. But you will find very few out there that can collect details about containers running at a given node, such as the number of running containers, container state, docker engine metrics, etc. cAdvisor is the best agent IMO for this job so far.

Awareness of continuous changes means that the monitoring pipeline is aware of different pods, containers instances and can relate them to their parent entities, i.e. Deployment, Statefulsets, Namespace, etc. It also means that the metrics server is aware of system-wide metrics that should be visible to users, such as the number of pending pods, nodes status, etc.
What about Metrics Visualization?

You can visualize metrics in many different ways. The most common open source tool that easily integrates with Prometheus is Grafana. The challenges you will face though is building proper dashboards to monitor the right metrics. That said, you should have dashboards monitoring the following:

- Cluster level capacity utilization, this shows how much CPU memory being across the whole cluster and per node.
- Kubernetes Orchestration Metrics, which tracks the status of your pods and containers inside your cluster. This includes the distribution of pods among nodes.
- Kubernetes Core Services, which visualizes the status of critical services such as CoreDNS, Calico, and any other service important for networking, storage, and pods scheduling.

- Application Specific Metrics, which tracks the status of your apps. They should reflect your users' experience and business critical metrics.

Note: You can get started with this Grafana template dashboards for Kubernetes.

- Grafana is not best suited for alerting. I see a lot of teams depend on it to create alerting rules. However, it is not as reliable and comprehensive as Prometheus alerting manager.

Changes To Watch For
Heapster is Going Away

Heapster is currently causing some confusion given that it is used to show both core pipeline metrics and services metrics. In reality, you can remove Heapster and nothing bad will happen to the core Kubernetes scheduling and orchestration scenarios. It was the default monitoring pipeline and I guess it still is the default in a lot of distributions. But you don't have to use it at all.

So, the Kubernetes community wanted to make the separation clearer between core and services monitoring pipelines. Hence, Heapster will be deprecated and replaced by the Metrics Server (MS) as the main source of aggregated core metrics. Think of the MS as a trimmed down version of Heapster. Major immediate changes are: (1) No historical data or queries, (2) eliminating a lot of container-specific metrics, pod focus metrics only. Metrics Server is meant to provide core metrics that are needed for core Kubernetes scenarios, such as autoscaling, scheduling,

etc., likely to take place in 2019 releases.
Metrics Server Will Get More Cool Features

Infrastore will store Metric Server historical data with a support of simple SQL-like queries. It will support initially metrics collected by the Metrics Server. My guess, because Kubernetes community love extensibility, they will make it extensible and allow custom metrics to be added to the Metrics Server and its store.

TL;DR

- You need to differentiate between core metrics pipeline and the services pipeline.
- Heapster will be deprecated. you should pick the best pipeline that works for your needs.
- The community official tool is Prometheus. You can use a variety of other open source or commercial tools, but I recommend to get started with Prometheus before you decide with any other tools that may cost you a lot down the road.
- Use Grafana for metrics visualization. But I wouldn't recommend using it for alerting.

TOP OPEN-SOURCE TOOLS FOR MONITORING KUBERNETES

Distributed computing and orchestration have solved many problems, but they also have created new challenges. While a Kubernetes cluster appears to a user to be a single computer, it is actually a set of independent nodes and multiple services that have been connected.

With this new way of building and running applications, your monitoring and observability strategies need to change—and so will the tools you use. Here are the most popular and most reliable open-source monitoring tools you can choose from when working with Kubernetes.

1. Kubelet

In a Kubernetes cluster, Kubelet acts as a bridge between the master and the nodes. It is the primary node agent that runs on each node and maintains a set of pods. Kubelet watches for PodSpecs via the Kubernetes API server and collects resource utilization statistics and pod and events status.

Kubelet fetches individual container usage statistics from Docker's Container Advisor (cAdvisor). But Kubelet also accepts PodSpecs provided through different mechanisms and ensures that the containers described in those PodSpecs are up and running. These aggregated pod resource usage statistics are exposed via a REST API.

2. Container Advisor (cAdvisor)

cAdvisor is a container resource usage and performance analysis agent; it's integrated into the Kubelet binary. cAdvistor auto-discovers all containers in a machine and collects statistics about memory, network usage, filesystem, and CPU. cAdvisor has native support for Docker containers. It does not operate at the pod level, but on each node.

Be advised, however: cAdvisor is a simple-to-use but limited tool, so if you are looking to store metrics for long-term use or perform complex monitoring actions, cAdvisor will not fit your needs.

3. Kube-state-metrics

Kube-state-metrics listens to the Kubernetes API server and generates metrics about the state of numerous Kubernetes objects, including cron jobs, config maps, pods, and nodes. These metrics are unmodified, unlike kubectl metrics that use the same Kubernetes API but apply some heuristics to display comprehensible and readable messages.

Kube-state-metrics uses the Golang Prometheus client to export metrics in the Prometheus metrics exposition format and expose metrics on an HTTP endpoint. Prometheus can consume the web endpoint.

This tool is not oriented toward performance and health but rather toward cluster-wide, state-based metrics such as the number of desired pod replicas for deployment or the total CPU resources available on a node.

4. Kubernetes Dashboard

Kubernetes Dashboard is a web-based, UI add-on for Kubernetes clusters. It has many features that allow users to create and manage workloads as well as do discovery, load balancing, configuration, storage, and monitoring. It is helpful for small clusters and for people starting to learn Kubernetes.

This tool offers different views for CPU and memory usage metrics aggregated across all nodes. It can also be used to monitor the health status of workloads (pods, deployments, replica sets, cron jobs, etc.). Installing Kubernetes Dashboard is quite easy and can be done using ready-to-use YAML files.

5. Prometheus

Prometheus is one of the most popular monitoring tools used with Kubernetes. It's community-driven and a member of the Cloud Native Computing Foundation. This project, developed first by SoundCloud and afterward donated to the CNCF, is inspired by Google Borg Monitor.

Prometheus stores all its data as a time series. This data can be queried via the PromQL query language and visualized with a built-in expression browser. Since Prometheus is not a dashboard, it relies on Grafana for visualizing data.

Version 1.0 of this tool was released in 2016, and it is becoming one of the most used Kubernetes monitoring tools. Other tools from the Kubernetes ecosystem, including Istio, include a built-in Prometheus adapter that exposes generated metrics.

Prometheus can be installed directly as a single binary that you can run on your host or as a Docker container. Running Prometheus on top of Kubernetes can be easily accomplished with the Prometheus Operator.

6. Jaeger

Jaeger is a tracing system released by Uber Technologies; it's used for troubleshooting and monitoring transactions in complex distributed systems.

With the rise of microservices and distributed systems, problems can include distributed context propagation, distributed transactions monitoring, and latency optimization. Jaeger addresses these problems as well as others that we can find in distributed systems.

Jaeger has native support for OpenTracing and addresses two main areas: networking and observability.

7. Kubewatch

Kubewatch is a Kubernetes watcher that publishes event notifications in a Slack channel. This tool allows you to specify the resources you want to monitor. It is written in Golang and uses a Kubernetes client library to interact with a Kubernetes API server.

Using a simple YAML file, you can choose the resources to watch, including daemon sets, deployments, pods, replica sets, replication controllers, services, secrets, and configuration maps.

8. Weave Scope

Weave Scope is a zero-configuration monitoring tool developed by Weaveworks. It generates a map of processes, containers, and hosts in a Kubernetes cluster to help understand Docker containers in real time. It can also be used to manage containers and run diagnostic commands on containers without leaving the graphical UI.

If you are looking for a practical graphical tool to obtain a visual overview of your Kubernetes cluster—including the application, the infrastructure, and the connections among your cluster nodes—Weave Scope may help you.

This tool is extensible via some plugins.

9. The EFK Stack

The EFK stack comprises Fluentd, Elasticsearch, and Kibana.

These tools work well with one another and together represent a reliable solution used for Kubernetes monitoring and log aggregation.

Fluentd collects logs from pods running on cluster nodes, then routes them to a centralized Elasticsearch. Then Elasticsearch ingests these logs from Fluentd and stores them in a central location. It is also used to efficiently search text files.

Kibana is the UI; the user can visualize the collected logs and metrics and create custom dashboards based on queries.

The EFK stack is useful for troubleshooting logs, dashboarding, and detecting issues as they come up—all in a user-friendly interface.

KUBERNETES MONITORING: BEST PRACTICES, METHODS, AND EXISTING SOLUTIONS

Monitoring an application's current state is one of the most effective ways to anticipate problems and discover bottlenecks in a production environment. Yet it is also currently one of the biggest challenges faced by almost all software development organizations. Deadlines, inexperience, culture, and management are just some of the obstacles that can affect how successful teams are at overcoming this challenge.

The growing adoption of microservices makes logging and monitoring more complex since a large number of applications, distributed and diversified in nature, are communicating with each other. A single point of failure can stop the entire process, but identifying it is becoming increasingly difficult.

Monitoring, of course, is just one challenge Microservices pose. Handling availability, performance, and deployments are pushing teams to create, or use, orchestrators to handle all the services and servers. There are several cluster orchestration tools, but Kubernetes (K8S) is becoming increasingly popular when compared to its competitors. A container orchestration tool such as Kubernetes handles containers in several computers, and removes the complexity of handling distributed processing.

But how does one monitor such a tool? There are so many variables to keep track of that we need new tools, new techniques, and new methods to effectively capture the data that matters.

Why Monitor Kubernetes and What Metrics Can Be Measured

As mentioned, Kubernetes is the most popular container orchestrator currently available. It is officially available in major clouds provided by Google, Azure, and, more recently AWS, and it can run in a local, bare metal data center. Even Docker has embraced Kubernetes and is now offering it as part of some of their packages.

Generally speaking, there are several Kubernetes metrics to monitor. These can be separated into two main components: (1) monitoring the cluster itself, and (2) monitoring pods.

Cluster Monitoring

For cluster monitoring, the objective is to monitor the health of the entire Kubernetes cluster. As an administrator, we are interested in discovering if all the nodes in the cluster are working properly and at what capacity, how many applications are running on each node, and the resource utilization of the entire cluster.

Allow me to highlight some of the measurable metrics:

- Node resource utilization – there are many metrics in this area, all related to resource utilization. Network bandwidth, disk utilization, CPU, and memory utilization are examples of this. Using these metrics, one can find out whether or not to increase or decrease the number and size of nodes in the cluster.
- The number of nodes – the number of nodes available is an important metric to follow. This allows you to figure out what you are paying for (if you are using cloud providers), and to discover

what the cluster is being used for.
- Running pods – the number of pods running will show you if the number of nodes available is sufficient and if they will be able to handle the entire workload in case a node fails.

Pod Monitoring

The act of monitoring a pod can be separated into three categories: (1) Kubernetes metrics, (2) container metrics, and (3) application metrics.

Using Kubernetes metrics, we can monitor how a specific pod and its deployment are being handled by the orchestrator. The following information can be monitored: the number of instances a pod has at the moment and how many were expected (if the number is low, your cluster may be out of resources), how the on-progress deployment is going (how many instances were changed from an older version to a new one), health checks, and some network data available through network services.

Container metrics are available mostly through Cadvisor and exposed by Heapster, which queries every node about the running containers. In this case, metrics like CPU, network, and memory usage compared with the maximum allowed are the highlights.

Finally, there are the application specific metrics. These metrics are developed by the application itself and are related to the business rules it addresses. For example, a database application will probably expose metrics related to an indices' state and statistics concerning tables and relationships. An e-commerce application would expose data concerning the number of users online and how much money the software made in the last hour, for example.

The metrics described in the latter type are commonly exposed directly by the application: if you want to keep closer track you should connect the application to a monitoring application.

Monitoring Kubernetes Methods

I'd like to mention two main approaches to collecting metrics from your cluster and exporting them to an external endpoint. As a guiding rule, the metric collection should be handled consistently over the entire cluster. Even if the system has nodes deployed in several places all over the world or in a hybrid cloud, the system should handle the metrics collection in the same way, with the same reliability.

Method 1 – Using DaemonSets

One approach to monitoring all cluster nodes is to create a special kind of Kubernetes pod called DaemonSets. Kubernetes ensures that every node created has a copy of the DaemonSet pod, which virtually enables one deployment to watch each machine in the cluster. As nodes are destroyed, the pod is also terminated. Many monitoring solutions use the DaemonSet structure to deploy an agent on every cluster node. In this case, there is not a general solution — each tool will have its own software for cluster monitoring.

Method 2 – Using Heapster

Heapster, on the other hand, is a uniform platform adopted by Kubernetes to generally send monitoring metrics to a system. Heapster is a bridge between a cluster and a storage designed to collect metrics. The supported storages are listed here.

Unlike DaemonSets, Heapster acts as a normal pod and discovers every cluster node via the Kubernetes API. Using Kubelet (a tool that enables master-node communications) and cAdvisor (a container monitoring tool that collects metrics for each running container), the bridge can store all relevant information about the cluster and its containers.

A cluster can consist of thousands of nodes, and an even greater amount of pods. It is virtually impossible to observe each one on a normal basis so it is important to create multiple labels for each deployment. For example, creating a label for database intensive pods will enable the operator to identify if there is a problem with the database service.
Comparing Monitoring Solutions

Let's take a look at five common monitoring solutions used by Kubernetes users. The first two tools (Heapster/InfluxDB/Grafana and Prometheus/Grafana) combine open source tools that are deployed inside Kubernetes. For the third option (Heapster/ELK) you can use your own ELK Stack or a hosted solution like Logz.io's. The last two options reviewed here (Datadog/Dynatrace) are proprietary APM solutions that provide Kubernetes monitoring.

The examples below are provided here. They use an Azure Container Service instance, but should work in any Kubernetes deployment without too many changes. As part of the testing process, a pod is deployed with a function randomly logging messages.

Heapster, InfluxDB, and Grafana

The most straightforward solution to monitor your Kubernetes cluster is by using a combination of Heapster to collect metrics, InfluxDB to store it in a time series database, and Grafana to present and aggregate the collected information.

The Heapster GIT project has the files needed to deploy this design.

Basically, as part of this solution, you'll deploy InfluxDB and Grafana, and edit the Heapster deployment to send data to InfluxDB. Use the command

Grafana is an extremely flexible tool and you can combine several metrics into a useful dashboard for yourself. In the example above, we captured the metrics provided by Kubernetes and Docker (via cAdvisor). They are generic metrics that every node and every pod will have, but you can also add specific metrics for applications.
Prometheus and Grafana

Prometheus is another popular solution for collecting Kubernetes metrics, with several tools, frameworks, and API's available for using it.

Since Prometheus does not have a Heapster sink, you can use InfluxDB and Prometheus together for the same Grafana instance, collecting different metrics, whenever each one is easier to collect.

Heapster + ELK Stack

The ELK Stack is a combination of three components: Elasticsearch, Logstash, and Kibana, each responsible for a different stage in the data pipeline. ELK is a widely used for centralized logging, but can also be used for collecting and monitoring metrics.

There are various methods of hooking in ELK with our Kubernetes. One method, for example, uses deploys fluentd as a DaemonSet. In the example below, however, we will simply create an Elasticsearch sink for Heapster.

Needless to say, the example above is an overly simple Elasticsearch instance that is not designed for scalability and high availability. And if you are monitoring a cluster, you should also consider not storing the data inside the same cluster as this will affect computed metrics, and you will not be able to investigate issues in case the cluster is down. A cloud-based ELK solution such as Logz.io can be used as a secure and reliable ELK endpoint that will automatically scale as your data grows.

Metricbeat is another ELK monitoring solution that is worth mentioning and will be reviewed in a future post. This solution involves installing Metricbeat on each monitored server to send metrics to Elasticsearch. A Kubernetes module for Metricbeat is still in the beta phase, but you can already use this shipper to monitor your cluster, nodes, and pods.

Datadog

Proprietary APM solutions like Datadog aim to simplify monitoring by enabling organizations to monitor their applications and infrastructure more easily. By definition, these systems are designed so that setting up a data pipeline is as effortless as possible, a simplicity that will often come at a cost.

To start using Datadog for monitoring your Kubernetes cluster, simply create an account, and access the Integrations → Agents area. Search for Kubernetes, and select the displayed result.

Dynatrace

Dynatrace is another APM solution that provides an agent that will run as a DaemonSet in your cluster. The steps to have a Dynatrace agent deployed are less straightforward since you have to collect data from more than one page until you have a proper deployment file.

Once you have the file deployed using

you'll have metrics flowing to Dynatrace in a few minutes.

Dynatrace does not distinguish between a simple Linux host and Kubernetes nodes, so you can't expect some useful Kubernetes metrics exposed by default like with Datadog.

THE STATE OF KUBERNETES CONFIGURATION MANAGEMENT: AN UNSOLVED PROBLEM

Configuration management is a hard, unsolved problem. When we first started Argo CD, a GitOps deployment tool for Kubernetes, we knew we had to limit its scope to a deployment tool and not go anywhere near config management. We understood that since there was no perfect config management solution, Argo CD should remain agnostic to how kubernetes manifests are rendered, and let the user decide for themselves the right tool and workflow that works best for them.

Good Kubernetes configuration tools have the following properties:

- Declarative. The config is unambiguous, deterministic and not system dependent.
- Readable. The config is written in a way that is easy to understand.
- Flexible. The tool helps facilitates, and does not get in the way of accomplishing what you are trying to do.
- Maintainable. The tool should promote reuse and composability.

A couple of key reasons Kubernetes config management is so challenging: what sounds like a simple act of deploying an application, can have wildly different, even opposing requirements, and it's difficult for a single tool to accommodate all such requirements. Imagine the following use cases:

A cluster operator who deploys 3rd-party, off-the-shelf applications, such as Wordpress, to their cluster with little to no customization of those apps. The most important criteria for this user is to easily receive updates from an upstream source and upgrade their application as easily and seamlessly as possible (e.g. new versions, security patches, etc...).

A SaaS application developer who deploys their bespoke application to one or more environments (e.g. dev, staging, prod-west, prod-east). These environments may be spread across different accounts, clusters, and namespaces with subtle differences between them, so configuration re-use is paramount. For these users, it is important to go from a Git commit in their code base to deploying to each of their environments in a fully automated way, and manage the configuration of their environments in a straightforward and maintainable way. These developers have zero interest in semantic versioning of their releases since they might be deploying multiple times a day, and the notion of a major, minor and patch versions ultimately have no meaning for their application.

As you can see, these are completely different use cases, and more often than not, a tool which excels at one, doesn't handle the other very well. After having built first class support in Argo CD for a few of the more popular config tools (Helm, kustomize, ksonnet, jsonnet), and having used these tools at Intuit to manage various applications in our clusters, we've accumulated some unique insights about the strengths and weaknesses of each.

Helm

Let's start with the obvious one, Helm, which needs no introduction. Love it or hate it, Helm, being the first one on the scene, is an integral part of the Kubernetes ecosystem, and chances are that at one point or another you've installed something by running helm install.

The important thing note about Helm is that it is a self-described package manager for Kubernetes, and doesn't claim to be a configuration management tool. However, since many people use Helm templating for exactly this purpose, it belongs in the discussion. These users invariably end up maintaining several values.yaml, one for each environment (e.g. values-base.yaml, values-prod.yaml, values-dev.yaml), then parameterize their chart in such a way that environment specific values can be used in the chart. This method more or less works, but it makes the templates unwieldy, since golang templating is flat, and needs to support every conceivable parameter for each environment, which ultimately litters the entire template with {{-if / else}} switches.

The Good:

There's a chart for that. Undoubtedly, Helm's biggest strength is its excellent chart repository. Just recently, we had the need to run a highly available Redis, without a persistent volume, to be used as a throwaway cache. There's something to be said about just being able to throw the redis-ha chart into your namespace, set persistentVolume.enabled: false, point your service at it, and someone else has already done the hard work of figuring out how to run Redis reliably on a Kubernetes cluster.

The Bad:

Golang templating. "Look that that beautiful and elegant helm template!", said no one ever. It is well known that Helm templates suffer from a readability problem. I don't doubt that this will be addressed with Helm 3's support for Lua, but until then, well, I hope you like curly braces.

Complicated SaaS CD pipelines. For SaaS CI/CD pipelines, assuming you are using Helm the way it is intended (i.e. using Tiller), an automated deploy in your pipeline might go several ways.

But in the worst case, where existing chart parameters cannot support your desired manifest changes, you go through a whole song and dance of bundling a new a Helm chart, bumping its semvers, publishing it to a chart repository, and redeploying with a helm upgrade. In the Linux world, this is analogous to building a new RPM, publishing the RPM to a yum repository, then running yum install, all so you can get your shiny new CLI into /usr/bin. While this model works great for packaging and distribution, in the case of bespoke SaaS applications, it's an unnecessarily complex and a roundabout way to deploy your applications. For this reason, many people choose to run helm template and pipe the output to kubectl apply, but at that point you are better off using some other tool that is specifically designed for this purpose.

Non-declarative by default. If you ever added --set param=value to any one of your Helm deploys, I'm sorry to tell you that your deployment process is not declarative. These values are only recorded in the Helm ConfigMap netherworld (and maybe your bash history), so hopefully you wrote those down somewhere. This is far from ideal if you ever need to recreate your cluster from scratch. A slightly better way would be to record all parameters in a new custom values.yaml which you can store in Git and deploy using -f my-values.yaml. However, this is annoying when you're deploying an OTS chart from Helm stable, and you don't have an obvious place to store that values.yaml side-by-side to the relevant chart. The best solution that I've come up with, is to compose a new dummy chart which has the upstream chart as a dependency. Still, I have yet to find a canonical way of updating a parameter in a values.yaml in a pipeline using a one-liner, short of running sed.

Kustomize

Kustomize was created around the design principles described in Brian Grant's excellent dissertation regarding Declarative Application Management. Kustomize has seen a meteoric rise in popularity, and in the eight months since it started, has already been merged into kubectl. Whether or not you agree with the manner in which it was merged, it goes without saying that kustomize applications will now have a permanent mainstay in the Kubernetes ecosystem and will be the default choice that users will gravitate towards for config management. Yes, it helps to be part of kubectl!
The Good:

No parameters & templates. Kustomize apps are extremely easy to reason about, and I dare say, a pleasure to look at. It's about as close as you can get to Kubernetes YAML since the overlays that you compose to perform customizations are basically subsets of Kubernetes YAML.

The Bad:

No parameters & templates. The same property that makes kustomize applications so readable, can also make it very limiting. For example, I was recently trying to get the kustomize CLI to set an image tag for a custom resource instead of a Deployment, but was unable to. Kustomize does have a concept of "vars," which look a lot like parameters, but somehow aren't, and can only be used in Kustomize's sanctioned whitelist of field paths. I feel like this is one of those times when the solution, despite making the hard things easy, ends up making the easy things hard.

Jsonnet

Jsonnet is actually a language and not really a "tool." Furthermore, its use is not specific to Kubernetes (although it's been popularized by Kubernetes). The best way to think of jsonnet is as super-powered JSON combined with a sane way to do templating. Jsonnet combines all the things you wish you could do with JSON (comments, text blocks, parameters, variables, conditionals, file imports), without any of the things that you hate about golang/Jinja2 templating, and adds features that you didn't even know you needed or wanted (functions, object orientation, mixins). It does all of this in a declarative and hermetic (code as data) way.

Jsonnet is not widely adopted in the Kubernetes community, which is unfortunate, because of all the tools described here, jsonnet is hands down the most powerful configuration tools available and is why several offshoot tools are built on-top of it. More on this later. Explaining what's possible with Jsonnet is a post in and of itself, which is why I encourage you to read how Databricks uses Jsonnet with Kubernetes, and Jsonnet's excellent learning tutorial.

The Good:

Extremely powerful. It's rare to hit a situation which couldn't be expressed in some concise and elegant snippet of jsonnet. With jsonnet, you are constantly finding new ways to maximize re-use and avoid repeating yourself.

The Bad:

It's not YAML. This might just be an issue with unfamiliarity, but most people will experience some level of cognitive load when they're staring at a non-trivial jsonnet file. In the same way that you would need to run helm template to verify your Helm chart is producing what you expect, you will similarly need to run jsonnet --yaml-stream guestbook.jsonnetto verify your jsonnet is correct. The good news is that, unlike golang templating which can produce syntactically incorrect YAML due to some misplaced whitespace, with jsonnet these type of errors are caught during build and the resulting output is guaranteed to be valid JSON/YAML.

Ksonnet (and other jsonnet derivatives)

Ksonnet (wordplay on the language for which it is based upon) was supposed to be the "jsonnet for Kubernetes." It provided an opinionated way to organize your jsonnet manifests into files & directories of "components" and "environments," backed by a CLI to help facilitate management of these files. Ksonnet made a big splash nearly two years ago when it was jointly announced by Heptio and Bitnami, working in conjunction with Microsoft and Box, a veritable who's who of the Kubernetes ecosystem. Fast forward to today, and ~~Heptio~~ VMware announces that the ksonnet project is now being sunsetted.

So what happened? Simply put, it was too hard to use. When starting with ksonnet, you were actually learning three things all at the same time: 1. the jsonnet language itself. 2. ksonnet's over-engineered concepts (components, prototypes, environments, parts, registries, modules). 3. ksonnet-lib, ksonnet's k8s jsonnet library. And if you were new to Kubernetes (as our dev teams were), make that four. Argo CD started with initial support for ksonnet and as someone who pushed for ksonnet adoption at Intuit, I am sorry to see it go. Despite my own efforts to make ksonnet easier for teams, I witnessed first-hand the continued struggles users faced with the tool.

Aside from ksonnet, there are a fair number of other jsonnet derived tools. These include kubecfg, kapitan, kasane, kr8. I don't have first-hand experience with them, but they are definitely worth a look.Ksonnet (and other jsonnet derivatives)

Ksonnet (wordplay on the language for which it is based upon) was supposed to be the "jsonnet for Kubernetes." It provided an opinionated way to organize your jsonnet manifests into files & directories of "components" and "environments," backed by a CLI to help facilitate management of these files. Ksonnet made a big splash nearly two years ago when it was jointly announced by Heptio and Bitnami, working in conjunction with Microsoft and Box, a veritable who's who of the Kubernetes ecosystem. Fast forward to today, and ~~Heptio~~ VMware announces that the ksonnet project is now being sunsetted.

So what happened? Simply put, it was too hard to use. When starting with ksonnet, you were actually learning three things all at the same time: 1. the jsonnet language itself. 2. ksonnet's over-engineered concepts (components, prototypes, environments, parts, registries, modules). 3. ksonnet-lib, ksonnet's k8s jsonnet library. And if you were new to Kubernetes (as our dev teams were), make that four. Argo CD started with initial support for ksonnet and as someone who pushed for ksonnet adoption at Intuit, I am sorry to see it go. Despite my own efforts to make ksonnet easier for teams, I witnessed first-hand the continued struggles users faced with the tool.

Aside from ksonnet, there are a fair number of other jsonnet derived tools. These include kubecfg, kapitan, kasane, kr8. I don't have first-hand experience with them, but they are definitely worth a look.

Replicated Ship

Ship, by replicated is relatively new to the scene, and focuses primarily on the problem of "last-mile customization" of third-party applications. It works by using both Helm and Kustomize to generate manifests. Why would you need to do this, you ask? Sooner or later, you will encounter a situation where a Helm chart is almost what you want, but you still need to tweak it somehow (e.g. add Network Policies, set Pod Affinity, etc…). After reviewing the built-in chart parameters, you realize that the chart doesn't provide an option for what you're trying to do. At this point people usually do one of two things: submit a PR upstream to add yet another parameter in the chart, or dump the contents of helm template into a file and hand-edit the YAML with their desired changes. The problem with the latter is that it's unmaintainable. When the time comes to get the latest from upstream, you can't easily discern or reapply the modifications you made in your fork. Ship solves this by keeping these separate: a tracking reference and staging directory hold the upstream helm chart, alongside your last-mile modifications written as kustomization overlays. Using this technique, the base manifests which you receive from upstream can be updated independently from your local kustomizations.

The Good:

It fills a gap. Ship makes it dead simple for operators to custom tailor a chart without having to a push change upstream. There's even a wonderful UI to help guide you through this process.

The Bad:

Only works for OTS. Ship is only intended to be used with an off-the-shelf, upstream source, which means it does not handle the bespoke application config use case at all.

We shouldn't need Ship. I find it unfortunate that we even need a tool like Ship. This is not a problem with Ship itself, but a commentary about the shortcomings of our current tools. Imagine, for example, if Helm provided a built-in way to apply simple overlays to upstream charts (as an alternative to parameters), we would end up with much simpler charts without the mess of overly parameterized templates. Another scenario is to imagine a world where everyone provided kustomize apps for their projects. If this was prevalent, then users could use kustomize's remote base feature to apply local changes against upstream kustomize apps. But unless either of those things happen, Ship is a tool to bridge that gap.

Helm 3 and Lua Script

I'm quite optimistic about the proposal for Helm 3 and its use of Lua based charts. Unfortunately, this aspect of Helm 3 is one of the least developed, and the maintainers have only just begun writing the underlying Lua VM which will power the rendering engine, so it will be quite some time before we'll have more readable charts. I do hope that they can address the last-mile customization gap, and be more friendly to GitOps style of deployments with the Helm 3 redesign.

Kubernetes configuration management is at an inflection point. With kustomize now readily available at user's fingertips, it is easier than ever to guide users towards an extremely capable configuration management out-of-the-box. But if there's a single takeaway from this discussion, it is that there is no perfect configuration management tool and they tend to come and go as the wind blows. Each tool will have its strengths and weaknesses, so it's important to understand when to use the right one for the job. At this moment, we have a mix of apps defined in kustomize, Helm, ksonnet, all in the same cluster for different reasons. With Argo CD, a guiding principle has been to provide users the most amount of flexibility in this regard, such as facilities to customize the repo server, and supporting the ability to execute custom commands to generate manifests.

The state of Kubernetes config management has never been more exciting (as exciting as writing text to generate more text can be :-). Kustomize's merge into kubectl changes the game entirely. Ksonnet's exit from the market is a sign of the space maturing. Jsonnet will always have a place for the power users. And while Helm has lost some community sentiment as of late with Tiller security concerns and template complexity, it does have a wildcard up its sleeve with Helm 3 and upcoming Lua charts. At the very least, Kubernetes configuration management is a rapidly evolving space which affects all Kubernetes users in some shape or form and everyone should have a vested interest in how things shape up in the years to come.

AN INTRODUCTION TO HELM, THE PACKAGE MANAGER FOR KUBERNETES

Introduction

Deploying applications to Kubernetes – the powerful and popular container-orchestration system – can be complex. Setting up a single application can involve creating multiple interdependent Kubernetes resources – such as pods, services, deployments, and replicasets – each requiring you to write a detailed YAML manifest file.

Helm is a package manager for Kubernetes that allows developers and operators to more easily package, configure, and deploy applications and services onto Kubernetes clusters.

Helm is now an official Kubernetes project and is part of the Cloud Native Computing Foundation, a non-profit that supports open source projects in and around the Kubernetes ecosystem.

In this ebook we will give an overview of Helm and the various abstractions it uses to simplify deploying applications to Kubernetes. If you are new to Kubernetes, it may be helpful to read An Introduction to Kubernetes first to familiarize yourself with the basics concepts.
An Overview of Helm

Most every programming language and operating system has its own package manager to help with the installation and maintenance of software. Helm provides the same basic feature set as many of the package managers you may already be familiar with, such as Debian's apt, or Python's pip.

Helm can:

- Install software.
- Automatically install software dependencies.
- Upgrade software.
- Configure software deployments.
- Fetch software packages from repositories.

Helm provides this functionality through the following components:

- A command line tool, helm, which provides the user interface to all Helm functionality.
- A companion server component, tiller, that runs on your Kubernetes cluster, listens for commands from helm, and handles the configuration and deployment of software releases on the cluster.
- The Helm packaging format, called charts.
- An official curated charts repository with prepackaged charts for popular open-source software projects.

We'll investigate the charts format in more detail next.

Charts

Helm packages are called charts, and they consist of a few YAML configuration files and some templates that are rendered into Kubernetes manifest files. Here is the basic directory structure of a chart:

These directories and files have the following functions:

- charts/: Manually managed chart dependencies can be placed in this directory, though it is typically better to use requirements.yaml to dynamically link dependencies.
- templates/: This directory contains template files that are combined with configuration values (from values.yaml and the command line) and rendered into Kubernetes manifests. The templates use the Go programming language's template format.
- Chart.yaml: A YAML file with metadata about the chart, such as chart name and version, maintainer information, a relevant website, and search keywords.
- LICENSE: A plaintext license for the chart.
- README.md: A readme file with information for users of the chart.
- requirements.yaml: A YAML file that lists the chart's dependencies.
- values.yaml: A YAML file of default configuration values for the chart.

The helm command can install a chart from a local directory, or from a .tar.gz packaged version of this directory structure. These packaged charts can also be automatically downloaded and installed from chart repositories or repos.

We'll look at chart repositories next.

Chart Repositories

A Helm chart repo is a simple HTTP site that serves an index.yaml file and .tar.gz packaged charts. The helm command has subcommands available to help package charts and create the required index.yaml file. These files can be served by any web server, object storage service, or a static site host such as GitHub Pages.

Helm comes preconfigured with a default chart repository, referred to as stable. This repo points to a Google Storage bucket at https://kubernetes-charts.storage.googleapis.com. The source for the stable repo can be found in the helm/charts Git repository on GitHub.

Alternate repos can be added with the helm repo add command. Some popular alternate repositories are:

- The official incubator repo that contains charts that are not yet ready for stable. Instructions for using incubator can be found on the official Helm charts GitHub page.
- Bitnami Helm Charts which provide some charts that aren't covered in the official stable repo.

- Whether you're installing a chart you've developed locally, or one from a repo, you'll need to configure it for your particular setup. We'll look into configs next.

Chart Configuration

A chart usually comes with default configuration values in its values.yaml file. Some applications may be fully deployable with default values, but you'll typically need to override some of the configuration to meet your needs.

The values that are exposed for configuration are determined by the author of the chart. Some are used to configure Kubernetes primitives, and some may be passed through to the underlying container to configure the application itself.

These are options to configure a Kubernetes Service resource. You can use helm inspect values chart-name to dump all of the available configuration values for a chart.

These values can be overridden by writing your own YAML file and using it when running helm install, or by setting options individually on the command line with the --set flag. You only need to specify those values that you want to change from the defaults.

A Helm chart deployed with a particular configuration is called a release. We will talk about releases next.

Releases

During the installation of a chart, Helm combines the chart's templates with the configuration specified by the user and the defaults in value.yaml. These are rendered into Kubernetes manifests that are then deployed via the Kubernetes API. This creates a release, a specific configuration and deployment of a particular chart.

This concept of releases is important, because you may want to deploy the same application more than once on a cluster. For instance, you may need multiple MySQL servers with different configurations.

You also will probably want to upgrade different instances of a chart individually. Perhaps one application is ready for an updated MySQL server but another is not. With Helm, you upgrade each release individually.

You might upgrade a release because its chart has been updated, or because you want to update the release's configuration. Either way, each upgrade will create a new revision of a release, and Helm will allow you to easily roll back to previous revisions in case there's an issue.

Creating Charts

If you can't find an existing chart for the software you are deploying, you may want to create your own. Helm can output the scaffold of a chart directory with helm create chart-name. This will create a folder with the files and directories we discussed in the Charts section above.

From there, you'll want to fill out your chart's metadata in Chart.yaml and put your Kubernetes manifest files into the templates directory. You'll then need to extract relevant configuration variables out of your manifests and into values.yaml, then include them back into your manifest templates using the templating system.

The helm command has many subcommands available to help you test, package, and serve your charts. For more information, please read the official Helm documentation on developing charts.

[Conclusion

We reviewed Helm, the package manager for Kubernetes. We overviewed the Helm architecture and the individual helm and tiller components, detailed the Helm charts format, and looked at chart repositories. We also looked into how to configure a Helm chart and how configurations and charts are combined and deployed as releases on Kubernetes clusters. Finally, we touched on the basics of creating a chart when a suitable chart isn't already available.

KUBERNETES HELM

Kubernetes HelmKubernetes Helm is a package manager for Kubernetes, analogous to Yum or Apt. It makes it possible to organize Kubernetes objects in a packaged application that anyone can download and install in one click, or configure to their specific needs. In Helm, these packages are called charts (similar to debs or rpms).

When a user installs a Helm chart, Helm deploys a Kubernetes cluster in the background, as specified in the chart's configuration.

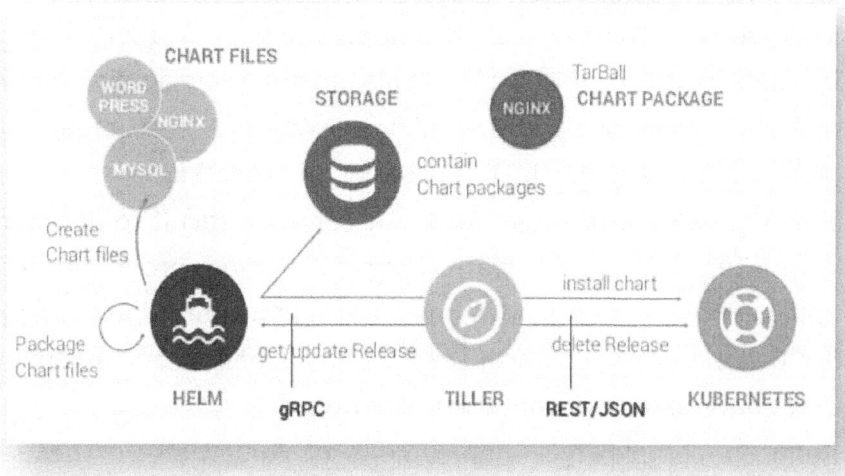

Helm is organized around several key concepts:

- A chart is a package of pre-configured Kubernetes resources
- A release is a specific instance of a chart which has been deployed to the cluster using Helm

- A repository is a group of published charts which can be made available to others

What Does Kubernetes Helm Solve?

Kubernetes is known as a complex platform with a steep learning curve. Kubernetes Helm helps make Kubernetes easier and faster to use:

- Improves productivity - instead of spending time on deploying test environments to test their Kubernetes clusters, developers can deploy a pre-tested app via a Helm chart and focus on developing their applications.
- Existing Helm Charts - allow developers to get a working database, big data platform, CMS, etc. deployed for their application with one click. Developers can modify existing charts or create their own to automate dev, test or production processes.
- Easier to start with Kubernetes - it can be difficult to get started with Kubernetes and learn how to deploy production-grade applications. Helm provides one click deployment of apps, making it much easier to get started and deploy your first app, even if you don't have extensive container experience.
- Reduced complexity - deployment of Kubernetes-orchestrated apps can be extremely complex. Using incorrect values in configuration files or failing to roll out apps correctly from YAML templates can break deployments. Helm Charts allow the community to preconfigure applications, defining values that are fixed and others that are configurable with sensible defaults, providing a consistent interface for changing configuration. This dramatically reduces complexity, and eliminates deployment

errors by locking out incorrect configurations.
- Production ready - running Kubernetes in production with all its components (pods, namespaces, deployments, etc.) is difficult and prone to error. With a tested, stable Helm chart, users can deploy to production with confidence, and reduce the complexity of maintaining a Kubernetes App Catalog.
- No duplicated effort - once a developer has created a chart, tested and stabilized it once, it can be reused across multiple groups in an organization and outside it. Previously, it was much more difficult (but not impossible) to share Kubernetes applications and replicate them between environments.

Kubernetes Helm Architecture

Helm consists of two main components:

- Helm Client - allows developers to create new charts, manage chart repositories, and interact with the tiller server.
- Tiller Server - runs inside the Kubernetes cluster. Interacts with Helm client, and translates chart definitions and configuration to Kubernetes API commands. Tiller combines a chart and its configuration to build a release. Tiller is also responsible for upgrading charts, or uninstalling and deleting them from the Kubernetes cluster.

- After Helm is installed, the helm init command installs the Tiller server to your running Kubernetes cluster. It is then possible to search for charts and install them to the cluster.

Chart Templates and Values

A Chart template is a mechanism by which the creator of the chart can define variables that users can modify when installing the chart. Those variables are called values, and the chart must define reasonable defaults for all values to ensure the chart installs correctly out of the box.

Chart templates are written in Go. All template files are stored in a chart's templates/ folder. When Helm accesses a chart, every file in that directory is rendered via the template engine.

To provide values for a template in a specific chart:

- You can provide a file called values.yaml inside of a chart, which contains default values.
- Chart users may supply a YAML file that contains values. This can be provided in the helm install command. User-provided values override the default values in the values.yaml file.

Hooks

Helm provides a hook mechanism, which allows a developer to intervene at specific points in a release's life cycle. The available hooks are:

- pre-install: after templates are rendered, but before resources created in Kubernetes.
- post-install: after all resources are loaded
- pre-delete: on deletion request before any resources are deleted
- post-delete: on a deletion request after all of the resources have

been deleted
- pre-upgrade: on an upgrade request after templates are rendered, before any resources are loaded
- post-upgrade: on an upgrade after all resources have been upgraded
- pre-rollback: on a rollback after templates are rendered, but before any resources have been rolled back
- post-rollback: on a rollback request after all resources have been modified

Technically, hooks are Kubernetes manifest files with special annotations in the metadata section. They are template files, so you can use all the regular template features. Here is an example of a job declared to be run on post-install:

Helm Repositories

A chart repository is a server that houses packaged charts. Any HTTP server that can serve YAML files and tar files can be used as a repository server. Helm does not provide tools for uploading charts to remote repository servers.

A repository has a special file called index.yaml that lists all the packages, together with data that allows retrieving and verifying those packages.

On the client side, repositories are managed with the helm repo commands.

HOW TO CREATE A KUBERNETES CLUSTER USING KUBEADM

Introduction

Kubernetes is a container orchestration system that manages containers at scale. Initially developed by Google based on its experience running containers in production, Kubernetes is open source and actively developed by a community around the world.

Kubeadm automates the installation and configuration of Kubernetes components such as the API server, Controller Manager, and Kube DNS. It does not, however, create users or handle the installation of operating-system-level dependencies and their configuration. For these preliminary tasks, it is possible to use a configuration management tool like Ansible or SaltStack. Using these tools makes creating additional clusters or recreating existing clusters much simpler and less error prone.

In this guide, you will set up a Kubernetes cluster from scratch using Ansible and Kubeadm, and then deploy a containerized Nginx application to it.

Goals

Your cluster will include the following physical resources:

One master node

The master node (a node in Kubernetes refers to a server) is responsible for managing the state of the cluster. It runs Etcd, which stores cluster data among components that schedule workloads to worker nodes.

Two worker nodes

Worker nodes are the servers where your workloads (i.e. containerized applications and services) will run. A worker will continue to run your workload once they're assigned to it, even if the master goes down once scheduling is complete. A cluster's capacity can be increased by adding workers.

After completing this guide, you will have a cluster ready to run containerized applications, provided that the servers in the cluster have sufficient CPU and RAM resources for your applications to consume. Almost any traditional Unix application including web applications, databases, daemons, and command line tools can be containerized and made to run on the cluster. The cluster itself will consume around 300-500MB of memory and 10% of CPU on each node.

Once the cluster is set up, you will deploy the web server Nginx to it to ensure that it is running workloads correctly.

Prerequisites

- An SSH key pair on your local Linux/macOS/BSD machine. If you haven't used SSH keys before, you can learn how to set them up by following this explanation of how to set up SSH keys on your local machine.

- Three servers running Ubuntu 18.04 with at least 1GB RAM. You should be able to SSH into each server as the root user with your SSH key pair.

- Ansible installed on your local machine. If you're running Ubuntu 18.04 as your OS, follow the "Step 1 - Installing Ansible" section in How to Install and Configure Ansible on Ubuntu 18.04 to install Ansible. For installation instructions on other platforms like macOS or CentOS, follow the official Ansible installation documentation.

- Familiarity with Ansible playbooks. For review, check out Configuration Management 101: Writing Ansible Playbooks.

- Knowledge of how to launch a container from a Docker image. Look at "Step 5 — Running a Docker Container" in How To Install and Use Docker on Ubuntu 18.04 if you need a refresher.

Step 1 — Setting Up the Workspace Directory and Ansible Inventory File

In this section, you will create a directory on your local machine that will serve as your workspace. You will configure Ansible locally so that it can communicate with and execute commands on your remote servers. Once that's done, you will create a hosts file containing inventory information such as the IP addresses of your servers and the groups that each server belongs to.

Out of your three servers, one will be the master with an IP displayed as master_ip. The other two servers will be workers and will have the IPs worker_1_ip and worker_2_ip.

Create a directory named ~/kube-cluster in the home directory of your local machine and cd into it:

This directory will be your workspace for the rest of the tutorial and will contain all of your Ansible playbooks. It will also be the directory inside which you will run all local commands.

Create a file named ~/kube-cluster/hosts using nano or your favorite text editor:

Add the following text to the file, which will specify information about the logical structure of your cluster:

You may recall that inventory files in Ansible are used to specify server information such as IP addresses, remote users, and groupings of servers to target as a single unit for executing commands. ~/kube-cluster/hosts will be your inventory file and you've added two Ansible groups (masters and workers) to it specifying the logical structure of your cluster.

In the masters group, there is a server entry named "master" that lists the master node's IP (master_ip) and specifies that Ansible should run remote commands as the root user.

Similarly, in the workers group, there are two entries for the worker servers (worker_1_ip and worker_2_ip) that also specify the ansible_user as root.

The last line of the file tells Ansible to use the remote servers' Python 3 interpreters for its management operations.

Save and close the file after you've added the text.

Having set up the server inventory with groups, let's move on to installing operating system level dependencies and creating configuration settings.

Step 2 — Creating a Non-Root User on All Remote Servers

In this section you will create a non-root user with sudo privileges on all servers so that you can SSH into them manually as an unprivileged user. This can be useful if, for example, you would like to see system information with commands such as top/htop, view a list of running containers, or change configuration files owned by root. These operations are routinely performed during the maintenance of a cluster, and using a non-root user for such tasks minimizes the risk of modifying or deleting important files or unintentionally performing other dangerous operations.

Create a file named ~/kube-cluster/initial.yml in the workspace:

Next, add the following play to the file to create a non-root user with sudo privileges on all of the servers. A play in Ansible is a collection of steps to be performed that target specific servers and groups. The following play will create a non-root sudo user:

Here's a breakdown of what this playbook does:

- Creates the non-root user ubuntu.

- Configures the sudoers file to allow the ubuntu user to run sudo commands without a password prompt.

- Adds the public key in your local machine (usually ~/.ssh/id_rsa.pub) to the remote ubuntu user's authorized key list. This will allow you to SSH into each server as the ubuntu user.

Save and close the file after you've added the text.

Next, execute the playbook by locally running:

Step 3 — Installing Kubernetetes' Dependencies

In this section, you will install the operating-system-level packages required by Kubernetes with Ubuntu's package manager. These packages are:

- Docker - a container runtime. It is the component that runs your containers. Support for other runtimes such as rkt is under active development in Kubernetes.

- kubeadm - a CLI tool that will install and configure the various components of a cluster in a standard way.

- kubelet - a system service/program that runs on all nodes and handles node-level operations.

- kubectl - a CLI tool used for issuing commands to the cluster through its API Server.

Create a file named ~/kube-cluster/kube-dependencies.yml in the workspace:

The first play in the playbook does the following:

- Installs Docker, the container runtime.

- Installs apt-transport-https, allowing you to add external HTTPS sources to your APT sources list.

- Adds the Kubernetes APT repository's apt-key for key verification.

- Adds the Kubernetes APT repository to your remote servers' APT sources list.

- Installs kubelet and kubeadm.

The second play consists of a single task that installs kubectl on your master node.

After execution, Docker, kubeadm, and kubelet will be installed on all of the remote servers. kubectl is not a required component and is only needed for executing cluster commands. Installing it only on the master node makes sense in this context, since you will run kubectl commands only from the master. Note, however, that kubectl commands can be run from any of the worker nodes or from any machine where it can be installed and configured to point to a cluster.

All system dependencies are now installed. Let's set up the master node and initialize the cluster.

Step 4 — Setting Up the Master Node

In this section, you will set up the master node. Before creating any playbooks, however, it's worth covering a few concepts such as Pods and Pod Network Plugins, since your cluster will include both.

A pod is an atomic unit that runs one or more containers. These containers share resources such as file volumes and network interfaces in common. Pods are the basic unit of scheduling in Kubernetes: all containers in a pod are guaranteed to run on the same node that the pod is scheduled on.

Each pod has its own IP address, and a pod on one node should be able to access a pod on another node using the pod's IP. Containers on a single node can communicate easily through a local interface. Communication between pods is more complicated, however, and requires a separate networking component that can transparently route traffic from a pod on one node to a pod on another.

This functionality is provided by pod network plugins. For this cluster, you will use Flannel, a stable and performant option.

Create an Ansible playbook named master.yml on your local machine:

Here's a breakdown of this play:

- The first task initializes the cluster by running kubeadm init. Passing the argument --pod-network-cidr=10.244.0.0/16 specifies the private subnet that the pod IPs will be assigned from. Flannel uses the above subnet by default; we're telling kubeadm to use the same subnet.

- The second task creates a .kube directory at /home/ubuntu. This directory will hold configuration information such as the admin key files, which are required to connect to the cluster, and the cluster's API address.

- The third task copies the /etc/kubernetes/admin.conf file that was generated from kubeadm init to your non-root user's home directory. This will allow you to use kubectl to access the newly-created cluster.

- The last task runs kubectl apply to install Flannel. kubectl apply -f descriptor.[yml|json] is the syntax for telling kubectl to create the objects described in the descriptor.[yml|json] file. The kube-flannel.yml file contains the descriptions of objects required for setting up Flannel in the cluster.

Save and close the file when you are finished.

The output states that the master node has completed all initialization tasks and is in a Ready state from which it can start accepting worker nodes and executing tasks sent to the API Server. You can now add the workers from your local machine.

Step 5 — Setting Up the Worker Nodes

Adding workers to the cluster involves executing a single command on each. This command includes the necessary cluster information, such as the IP address and port of the master's API Server, and a secure token. Only nodes that pass in the secure token will be able join the cluster.

Navigate back to your workspace and create a playbook named workers.yml:

Here's what the playbook does:

- The first play gets the join command that needs to be run on the worker nodes. This command will be in the following format:kubeadm join --token <token> <master-ip>:<master-port> --discovery-token-ca-cert-hash sha256:<hash>. Once it gets the actual command with the proper token and hash values, the task sets it as a fact so that the next play will be able to access that info.

- The second play has a single task that runs the join command on all worker nodes. On completion of this task, the two worker nodes will be part of the cluster.

Save and close the file when you are finished.

Execute the playbook by locally running:

With the addition of the worker nodes, your cluster is now fully set up and functional, with workers ready to run workloads. Before scheduling applications, let's verify that the cluster is working as intended.

Step 6 — Verifying the Cluster

A cluster can sometimes fail during setup because a node is down or network connectivity between the master and worker is not working correctly. Let's verify the cluster and ensure that the nodes are operating correctly.

You will need to check the current state of the cluster from the master node to ensure that the nodes are ready. If you disconnected from the master node, you can SSH back into it with the following command:

If all of your nodes have the value Ready for STATUS, it means that they're part of the cluster and ready to run workloads.

If, however, a few of the nodes have NotReady as the STATUS, it could mean that the worker nodes haven't finished their setup yet. Wait for around five to ten minutes before re-running kubectl get nodes and inspecting the new output. If a few nodes still have NotReady as the status, you might have to verify and re-run the commands in the previous steps.

Now that your cluster is verified successfully, let's schedule an example Nginx application on the cluster.

Step 7 — Running An Application on the Cluster

You can now deploy any containerized application to your cluster. To keep things familiar, let's deploy Nginx using Deployments and Services to see how this application can be deployed to the cluster. You can use the commands below for other containerized applications as well, provided you change the Docker image name and any relevant flags (such as ports and volumes).

Still within the master node, execute the following command to create a deployment named nginx:

A deployment is a type of Kubernetes object that ensures there's always a specified number of pods running based on a defined template, even if the pod crashes during the cluster's lifetime. The above deployment will create a pod with one container from the Docker registry's Nginx Docker Image.

Next, run the following command to create a service named nginx that will expose the app publicly. It will do so through a NodePort, a scheme that will make the pod accessible through an arbitrary port opened on each node of the cluster:

Services are another type of Kubernetes object that expose cluster internal services to clients, both internal and external. They are also capable of load balancing requests to multiple pods, and are an integral component in Kubernetes, frequently interacting with other components.

Run the following command:

From the third line of the above output, you can retrieve the port that Nginx is running on. Kubernetes will assign a random port that is greater than 30000 automatically, while ensuring that the port is not already bound by another service.

To test that everything is working, visit http://worker_1_ip:nginx_port or http://worker_2_ip:nginx_port through a browser on your local machine. You will see Nginx's familiar welcome page.

If you would like to remove the Nginx application, first delete the nginx service from the master node:

Conclusion

In this guide, you've successfully set up a Kubernetes cluster on Ubuntu 18.04 using Kubeadm and Ansible for automation.

If you're wondering what to do with the cluster now that it's set up, a good next step would be to get comfortable deploying your own applications and services onto the cluster. Here's a list of links with further information that can guide you in the process:

- Dockerizing applications - lists examples that detail how to containerize applications using Docker.

- Pod Overview - describes in detail how Pods work and their relationship with other Kubernetes objects. Pods are ubiquitous in Kubernetes, so understanding them will facilitate your work.

- Deployments Overview - provides an overview of deployments. It is useful to understand how controllers such as deployments work since they are used frequently in stateless applications for scaling and the automated healing of unhealthy applications.

- Services Overview - covers services, another frequently used object in Kubernetes clusters. Understanding the types of services and the options they have is essential for running both stateless and stateful applications.

Other important concepts that you can look into are Volumes, Ingresses and Secrets, all of which come in handy when deploying production applications.

Kubernetes has a lot of functionality and features to offer. The Kubernetes Official Documentation is the best place to learn about concepts, find task-specific guides, and look up API references for various objects.

DEPLOY, SCALE AND UPGRADE AN APPLICATION ON KUBERNETES WITH HELM

Introduction

Containers have revolutionized application development and delivery on account of their ease of use, portability and consistency. And when it comes to automatically deploying and managing containers in the cloud (public, private or hybrid), one of the most popular options today is Kubernetes.

Kubernetes is an open source project designed specifically for container orchestration. Kubernetes offers a number of key features, including multiple storage APIs, container health checks, manual or automatic scaling, rolling upgrades and service discovery. Applications can be installed to a Kubernetes cluster via Helm charts, which provide streamlined package management functions.

If you're new to Kubernetes and Helm charts, one of the easiest ways to discover their capabilities is with Bitnami. Bitnami offers a number of stable, production-ready Helm charts to deploy popular software applications, such as WordPress, Magento, Redmine and many more, in a Kubernetes cluster. Or, if you're developing a custom application, it's also possible to use Bitnami's Helm charts to package and deploy it for Kubernetes.

This guide walks you through the process of bootstrapping an example MongoDB, Express, Angular and Node.js (MEAN) application on a Kubernetes cluster. It uses a custom Helm chart to create a Node.js and MongoDB environment and then clone and deploy a MEAN application from a public Github repository into that environment. Once the application is deployed and working, it also explores some of Kubernetes' most interesting features: cluster scaling, load-balancing, and rolling updates.

Assumptions and Prerequisites

This guide focuses on deploying an example MEAN application in a Kubernetes cluster running on either Google Container Engine (GKE) or Minikube. The example application is a single-page Node.js and MongoDB to-do application available on Github.

This guide makes the following assumptions:

- You have a Kubernetes 1.5.0 (or later) cluster.
- You have kubectl installed and configured to work with your Kubernetes cluster.
- You have git installed and configured.
- You have a basic understanding of how containers work.

Step 1: Validate the Kubernetes cluster

First, ensure that you are able to connect to your cluster with kubectl cluster-info. This command is also a good way to get the IP address of your cluster.

Step 2: Install Helm and Tiller

To install Helm, execute these commands:

Step 3: Deploy the example application

The smallest deployable unit in Kubernetes is a "pod". A pod consists of one or more containers which can communicate and share data with each other. Pods make it easy to scale applications: scale up by adding more pods, scale down by removing pods. Learn more about pods.

The Helm chart used in this guide deploys the example to-do application as two pods: one for Node.js and the other for MongoDB. This is considered a best practice because it allows a clear separation of concerns, and it also allows the pods to be scaled independently (you'll see this in the next section).

To deploy the sample application using a Helm chart, follow these steps:

- Clone the Helm chart from Bitnami's Github repository:
- Check for and install missing dependencies with helm dep. The Helm chart used in this example is dependent on the MongoDB chart in the official repository, so the commands below will take care of identifying and installing the missing dependency.
- Lint the chart with helm lint to ensure it has no errors.
- Deploy the Helm chart with helm install. This will produce two pods (one for the Node.js service and the other for the MongoDB service). Pay special attention to the NOTES section of the output, as it contains important information to access the application.

Get the URL for the Node application by executing the commands shown in the output of helm install, or by using helm status my-todo-app and checking the output for the external IP address.

If you deployed the application on GKE, use these commands to obtain the URL for the Node application:

If you deployed the application on Minikube, use these commands instead to obtain the URL for the Node application:

Browse to the specified URL and you should see the sample application running. Here's what it should look like:

To debug and diagnose deployment problems, use kubectl get pods -l app=my-todo-app-mean. If you specified a different release name (or didn't specify one), remember to use the actual release name from your deployment.

To delete and reinstall the Helm chart at any time, use the helm delete command, shown below. The additional --purge option removes the release name from the store so that it can be reused later.

Step 4: Explore Kubernetes and Helm
Scale up (or down)

As more and more users access your application, it becomes necessary to scale up in order to handle the increased load. Conversely, during periods of low demand, it often makes sense to scale down to optimize resource usage.

Kubernetes provides the kubectl scale command to scale the number of pods in a deployment up or down.

A key feature of Kubernetes is that it is a self-healing system: if one or more pods in a Kubernetes cluster are terminated unexpectedly, the cluster will automatically spin up replacements. This ensures that the required number of pods are always running at any given time.

As you can see, this cluster has been scaled up to have 2 Node.js pods. Now, select one of the Node.js pods and simulate a pod failure by deleting it with a command like the one below. Replace the POD-ID placeholder with an actual pod identifier from the output of the kubectl get pods command.

If you keep watching the output of kubectl get pods -w, you will see the state of the new pod change rapidly from "Pending" to "Running".

Balance traffic between pods

It's easy enough to spin up two (or more) replicas of the same pod, but how do you route traffic to them? When deploying an application to a Kubernetes cluster in the cloud, you have the option of automatically creating a cloud network load balancer (external to the Kubernetes cluster) to direct traffic between the pods. This load balancer is an example of a Kubernetes Service resource. Learn more about services in Kubernetes.

You've already seen a Kubernetes load balancer in action. When deploying the application to GKE with Helm, the command used the serviceType option to create an external load balancer,

When invoked in this way, Kubernetes will not only create an external load balancer, but will also take care of configuring the load balancer with the internal IP addresses of the pods, setting up firewall rules, and so on. To see details of the load balancer service, use the kubectl describe svc command,

Notice the LoadBalancer Ingress field, which specifies the IP address of the load balancer, and the Endpoints field, which specifies the internal IP addresses of the three Node.js pods in use. Similarly, the Port field specifies the port that the load balancer will listen to for connections (in this case, 80, the standard Web server port) and the NodePort field specifies the port on the internal cluster node that the pod is using to expose the service.

Obviously, this doesn't work quite the same way on a Minikube cluster running locally. Look back at the Minikube deployment and you'll see that the serviceType option was set to NodePort. This exposes the service on a specific port on every node in the cluster.

The main difference here is that instead of an external network load balancer service, Kubernetes creates a service that listens on each node for incoming requests and directs it to the static open port on each endpoint.

Perform rolling updates (and rollbacks)

Rolling updates and rollbacks are important benefits of deploying applications into a Kubernetes cluster. With rolling updates, devops teams can perform zero-downtime application upgrades, which is an important consideration for production environments. By the same token, Kubernetes also supports rollbacks, which enable easy reversal to a previous version of an application without a service outage.

By now, you should have a good idea of how some of the key features available in Kubernetes, such as scaling and automatic load balancing, work. You should also have an appreciation for how Helm charts make it easier to perform common actions in a Kubernetes deployment, including installing, upgrading and rolling back applications.

KUBERNETES DEPLOYMENT

Kubernetes has exploded in growth over the past few years because of its powerful abilities to manage containers in production. While it's easy to spin up your first container locally, taking containers into production in a cloud environment is a completely different ball game. There are numerous aspects like scale, networking, security, high availability, and performance that need to be considered. All of these factors come into play when deploying containers. This makes deployment the most stressful part of running containers in production. Fortunately, Kubernetes is a mature and robust option for running containers in production and has some strong defaults, wide-ranging options, and is a complete package when looking for a tool to deploy containerized applications.

Key Components of Kubernetes

To understand the Kubernetes approach to deployment you need to know the various components that work together.

Pod

A pod is a group of containers that share common resources like networking and storage and are located on the same node.

ReplicaSet

A ReplicaSet ensures that all pods have a required number of replicas running at any given time.

DaemonSet

A DaemonSet ensures that all active nodes are running at least one pod. It dynamically allocates pods on nodes as they are created and removed.

Deployment

In Kubernetes, a deployment is a feature that manages pods and ReplicaSets. In other words, as you trigger a release the Deployment controller updates the pods and ReplicaSets by making changes to them or replacing them with newly updated pods and ReplicaSets.

Helm

Helm is growing in popularity as a package manager for Kubernetes. It helps manage charts, which are packages of pre-configured Kubernetes resources. Helm can find and install popular software packaged as Kubernetes charts, share applications as Kubernetes charts, create reproducible builds, manage Kubernetes manifest files and releases used for packages.

DockerHub can also automatically scan images in private repositories for vulnerabilities, producing a report detailing vulnerabilities found in each image layer, by severity (critical, major or minor).

Note that multiple private repos, parallel builds and image security scanning are only available with paid subscriptions.
Common Deployment Tasks

Execute a Deployment

To initiate a deployment you need to create a YAML file with the specifications for the deployment using the kubectl create command.
Rollback During a Deployment

Kubernetes always records the change history for deployments in the pod template file. If a deployment has issues and you want to revert to an older version while a deployment is in progress you need to run the rollback command which will stop the existing deployment and start reverting back to the old replicas. This is possible because of the way Kubernetes scales replicas up and down during a deployment.

If you've labeled your previous deployments, you can even rollback to a specific previous deployment.

Kubernetes also lets you pause a rollout, update any images that are part of that deployment, and then resume the rollout. This way you can reduce the number of rollouts.

Phases of a Deployment

Kubernetes has multiple phases for a deployment. A deployment can be in progress, complete, or failed. You can view the state of a deployment by running the kubectl rollout status command.

A deployment can fail due to many reasons such as resource constraints, image pull errors, inadequate permissions and more.

Clean-up After a Deployment

After every deployment Kubernetes automatically checks for previous replicas that can be deleted. You specify how many past versions you'd like to keep using the .spec.revisionHistoryLimit field. The default value is 2, and if you set it to 0 all older replicas will be deleted. But ideally, you want to keep some of the older replicas in case you'd like to rollback any deployment.

Deployment Commands

- Create a deployment based on a YAML file

- kubectl create

- Deploy using a phased rolling update

- kubectl rollout

- Check the status of a rolling update

- kubectl rollout status

- Rollback a recent or ongoing rolling update to a previous version

- kubectl rollback

- Option to delete old replicas

- .spec.revisionHistoryLimit

Deployment Strategies

There are many approaches to deployment in Kubernetes ranging from the simple to the complex.

Recreate Deployment

In this approach all replicas are killed, and are then replaced by new replicas. It involves some downtime for as long as it takes for the system to shut down and boot up again. This works fine for applications that are used infrequently, and where users don't expect them to be available 24x7. This is rare in today's cloud-driven world, and hence, this isn't the most popular deployment method.

Rolling Update

By default Kubernetes takes a phased approach to updates. When a deployment command is executed, Kubernetes starts to replace existing replicas with the new updated ones one at a time. This scaling up and scaling down of replicas is how Kubernetes manages deployments, and is what makes Kubernetes particularly effective at managing deployments with containers. As discussed earlier, you can rollback a rolling update even when it's in progress.

Blue-green Deployments

Blue green deployments are not native to Kubernetes, but you can set them up with ease. In this method the 'blue' replicas are the existing instances, and they are to be replaced by the 'green' replicas.

First, You setup Deployments to rollout the green replicas alongside the blue ones. This would take additional resources to run both the old and new deployments, but not for long. Once the green replicas are deployed and tested, you can use an external load balancer to route traffic from the 'blue' replicas to the 'green' ones. Tools like Linkerd allow for advanced load balancing so you can define how much and which kind of traffic you'd like to route to which replicas. The biggest advantage of blue-green deployments is that it ensures a smooth transition without any downtime.

Canary Releases

A canary release is when you release a new version of the app to a subset of users, say 5% of all users. Once this version is tested and reliable for the initial 5% it is released to a bigger subset, until eventually all users get updated to the release without experiencing any downtime.

The biggest advantage of canary releases is that they enable you to test the app in real-world conditions and with real users. This brings a big boost in productivity. However, it does take some upfront planning and management along the way to ensure the release is seamless from a user experience point of view.

On the Kubernetes blog, Bitmovin has written about how they implement multi-stage canary deployments. They go into more detail about this type of deployment strategy

Conclusion

Kubernetes is built to manage containers in production, and this is evident in the powerful features it has for deployments. It makes deployments easy by allowing you to control then using a simple YAML configuration file. It can do vanilla deployments where old versions are deleted and replaced by new ones, or it can take more mature approaches like rolling updates, blue-green deployments, and canary releases. You can experiment and find out which best suits your application. By understanding the various Kubernetes components involved in a deployment, and the many options at your disposal, you are now ready to take your Kubernetes deployments to the next level.

KUBERNETES SERVICES

What is a Service in Kubernetes?

For Kubernetes, a service is an abstraction that represents a set of logical pods where an application or component is running, as well as embedding an access policy to those pods. Actual pods are ephemeral, Kubernetes guarantees the availability of pods and replicas specified but not the liveliness of each individual pod. This means that other pods that need to communicate with this application or component cannot rely on the underlying individual pod's IP addresses.

A service gets allocated a virtual IP address as well (called a clusterIP in Kubernetes), and lives until explicitly destroyed. Requests to the service get redirected to the appropriate pods, thus the service serves as a stable endpoint used for inter-component or application communication. For Kubernetes-native applications, requests can also be made via an API in Kubernetes' apiserver which automatically exposes and maintains the actual pods endpoints at any moment.

Specifying Pods in a Service

A service in Kubernetes can be created via an API request by passing in a service definition such as:

kind: Service
apiVersion: v1
metadata:
  name: my-service

```
spec:
  selector:
    app: MyApp
  ports:
   - protocol: TCP
     port: 80
     targetPort: 9376
```

In this example the new service is named my-service and will target TCP port 9376 on any pod with the metadata label "app=MyApp" . Kubernetes constantly evaluates the service's label selector to determine at any given moment which pods are included in the service. This means that a new service can include existing pods that already match the label selector.

To facilitate port changes in the pods/applications, Kubernetes supports strings for targetPorts, so each pod in the service can expose a different port, as long as there's a mapping to a commonly named port. This allows, for example, to change the port number that pods expose in the next version of your backend software, without breaking clients.

Using Services for External Workloads

A service can apply to an external workload as well, allowing to use the same abstraction to connect to a backend or database running outside Kubernetes, for example. Pods can then connect to this service and without knowing about specific endpoints for workloads outside of Kubernetes.

In order to do so the service should be defined as in previous section but without the label selector. After the service is created, the endpoints for the external workload need to be specified. For example:

kind: Endpoints
apiVersion: v1
metadata:
 name: my-service
subsets:
 - addresses:
 - ip: 62.82.24.195
 ports:
 - port: 9376

All incoming traffic to my-service will get routed straight through to endpoint 62.82.24.195:9376

Service Types

The default and simplest service type is ClusterIP . It exposes the service's ClusterIP address internally to the Kubernetes cluster. Other types allow different access policies to the service and include:

- NodePort - exposes the service on the specified port number, on all nodes in the Kubernetes cluster. Meaning that an incoming request to a node's IP on the specified port will get routed to the service's ClusterIP .

- LoadBalancer - service is exposed like in NodePort but creates a load balancer in the cloud where Kubernetes is running (if supported by the cloud provider) that receives external requests to the service. It then distributes them among the cluster nodes using NodePort. To specify this type add this line to the spec:

- type: LoadBalancer

- ExternalName - returns an alias to an external component residing outside the Kubernetes cluster. An incoming request for the service gets routed by Kubernetes DNS to the external domain specified. For example, to redirect traffic sent to my-service to my.database.example.com :

kind: Service
apiVersion: v1
metadata:
  name: my-service
  namespace: default
spec:
  type: ExternalName
  externalName: my.database.example.com

Service Discovery

Service discovery in Kubernetes can be achieved via the cluster DNS (recommended) or via environment variables on the nodes.

The DNS server watches the Kubernetes API for new services and creates a set of DNS records for each. Pods can then access services via standard DNS name resolution. If namespaces are being used in the cluster, then pods outside need to qualify the namespace of the service, for example by calling my-service.my-namespace instead of just my-service .

Environment variables are less reliable as a pod might fail to reach a service that was created after the pod. Kubernetes exports a set of environment variables for each service currently active in the Kubernetes cluster at pod creation time. These variables are exported on the node where the pod gets created, so they become visible to the pod. For example, these variables (and more) would get exported for each of the active services payments and orders:

PAYMENTS_SERVICE_HOST=10.0.0.11
PAYMENTS_SERVICE_PORT=6379
ORDERS_SERVICE_HOST=10.0.171.239
ORDERS_SERVICE_PORT=6379

But if the orders service did not exist yet at pod creation time, then orders would not be visible to the pod through environment variables.

Multi-Cluster Services with Cluster Federation

Kubernetes Cluster Federation allows a (federated) service to run on multiple Kubernetes clusters simultaneously. The clusters can be spread across different cloud providers, availability zones and even private clouds, as long as the cluster's API endpoint and credentials are registered with the Federation API server.

A new federated service can be created by calling the Federation API in the same manner as a cluster-specific kube-apiserver would be called for a (non-federated) service (as described in this article up to now). Federation means that the service will be sharded across all the Kubernetes clusters that are part of the federation.

A pod can access a federated service in a similar fashion to a regular service, by adding the federation name. For example calling my-service.my-namespace.my-federation gets automatically resolved by Kubernetes DNS server to the (geographically) nearest cluster where the service is running (under normal circumstances this would be service shard in the same cluster where the pod resides).

The health of the service in each cluster is automatically monitored and a set of DNS records is kept up-to-date accordingly. Such records are set up in an hierarchical way. For example, a request sent to the top-level record:

my-service.mynamespace.my-federation.svc.example.com

could get forwarded to any (healthy) service endpoint on any of the federated clusters (on any zone, region or provider). However, a request sent to

my-service.my-namespace.my-federation.svc.europe-west1-d.example.com

will get forwarded to an endpoint in a cluster inside availability zone europe-west1-d.

Should there be no healthy service shard running in that zone, the request will get forwarded to a cluster on another availability zone in the europe-west1 region, Should that still fail to reach a healthy service, then the request would get forwarded to the top-level:

my-service.mynamespace.my-federation.svc.example.com

and possibly get handled by a service shard in a different region or even a different cloud provider.

Federation provides high availability of services, availability zone fault tolerance and built-in service discovery across multiple zones, regions, providers and on-premise clusters.

Common operations with kubectl

The kubectl c ommand line makes it easier to run some common operations with Kubernetes services:

- Create a service - It's possible to specify that all deployed pods in a given deployment are part of a new service. For example this command will create service my-nginx which targets TCP port 80 on any pod with the run: my-nginx metadata label:

- $ kubectl expose deployment/my-nginx

- Describe a service - This is useful to check that the service was created as expected or to find out its ClusterIP or the endpoints of the pods currently part of the service. To describe service my-nginx :

- $ kubectl describe svc my-nginx

- List all services - For a full list of services running in the cluster, run kubectl get services

- Check if Kubernetes DNS service is running : The DNS service must be up and running for service discovery via name resolution to work. To check if it's running in a cluster run:

- $ kubectl get services kube-dns --namespace=kube-system

- Remove a service - kubectl delete is the command for deleting Kubernetes resources. For example, to remove service my-nginx run:

- $ kubectl delete svc my-nginx

KUBERNETES ON AWS

Overview

Amazon Web Services (AWS) is a popular cloud provider option for Kubernetes deployments, as it allows unlimited scaling of an enterprise containerized application clusters. AWS' region availability all around the world means Kubernetes clusters can benefit from very low latencies. Additionally, the wide range of AWS services like S3 for raw storage or RDS for relational databases, it becomes easy to use Kubernetes for both stateless and stateful workloads integrated with native AWS services.

Kubernetes Components and Architecture

A Kubernetes node runs the kube-proxy and kubelet components together with a container runtime engine, typically Docker.

1. kube-proxy

This Kubernetes proxy service runs on each node in the cluster and works as a load balancer for services running on a single worker node. Proxy service watches the master node for addition and removal of services/endpoints and does load balancing via simple UDP, TCP stream forwarding and round-robin across a set of backend services. The proxy service is also responsible for virtual IP implementation for regular services.

2. kubelet

kubelet is the lowest level component of Kubernetes that runs on each node in the cluster, it's kind of a process watcher for containers. kubelet works on pod object specifications. Since those declare a desired state, kubelet works to make sure that the current state matches the desired state.

3. cAdvisor

cAdvisor is responsible for collecting, aggregating, processing and exporting metrics for instance memory, CPU and network data among others about containers that are running on a certain node. It has a built-in web interface as well to visualize the metrics.

Kubernetes vs. ECS

Here we'll look at the differences between deploying and running your own Kubernetes clusters (for example on AWS EC2 instances) versus AWS ECS service, Amazon's own container orchestration service. Both options present advantages and disadvantages, depending on which use case and operational requirements.

ECS is a highly scalable, high performance container orchestration service that supports Docker and allows running and scaling containerized applications on AWS with minimal configuration.

Ease of Setup

Tools like kops or kubeadm can greatly ease the task of deploying a Kubernetes cluster on AWS EC2. These tools make extensive use of AWS' APIs to automate the process.

On the other hand, for those who prefer a GUI, setting up an ECS cluster via AWS' dashboard is quite straightforward.

Networking

Kubernetes has a built-in service discovery with a particular networking model which automatically assigns a new IP address to every pod. Also, a new subnet gets created for each new Kubernetes node. However, multi-availability zones (multi-AZ) support poses a challenge as a single Kubernetes cluster cannot spread across multiple availability zones. Instead, to support that use case, one must use Kubernetes federation model with multiple clusters that must register themselves in the federation.

On the other hand, ECS has built-in service discovery which integrates natively with AWS Elastic Load Balancing (ELB) and Application Load Balancers. Each container created on ECS gets a new port number, requiring application awareness of those ports. Finally, there are no scaling issues for ECS between regions and availability zones since this feature is natively managed by AWS.

Vendor Lock-in

Given Kubernetes' community and open source nature, it naturally supports multiple cloud vendors (despite its Google origins) and even bare metal implementations. A given Kubernetes configuration is mostly portable between providers. However, when the applications running on Kubernetes are deeply integrated with AWS or other cloud services, that will increase the complexity of migrating to a different cloud provider. Note that this is not much different from migrating a regular application running on a cloud provider without Kubernetes.

On the other hand, ECS is a native AWS service, thus it can only run clusters and containers on AWS cloud. So in essence this locks in the applications to the AWS ecosystem as the ECS container setup cannot be easily migrated to another cloud provider or on-premises.

Fault Tolerance and Orchestrator Resilience

Kubernetes provides fault tolerance at the pod and container level, so if one containerized application fails it will be automatically restarted. To ensure orchestrator resiliency (VM-level fault tolerance), you can use Autoscaling Groups so AWS will automatically restart crashed VM instances and ensure a target number of instances is maintained. It is a good practice to put all master instances in one autoscaling group to ensure a quorum is maintained. The same can be done for worker nodes.

On the other hand, ECS transparently manages your cluster and ensures it is highly available. If a node in the cluster goes down, it will automatically be re-created and brought back to service. You only intervene when you want to change your physical setup, either growing or reducing the cluster size.

Third-party Tools

A growing number of third party tools (for example for DNS management or networking) developed by the community are available to extend Kubernetes functionalities.

On the other hand, although ECS provides a rich set of APIs, it is still a closed platform, thus not as prone to extensions via third party tools. Requests for new features and bug fixes will depend on Amazon's roadmap and priorities.

Which One to Choose?

ECS excels when it comes to ease of deployment and maintenance. ECS does all the work behind the scenes. ECS is ideal for quick setup and providing multi-AZ HA out-of-the-box.

On the other hand, Kubernetes provides the flexibility to migrate or share the same configuration between on-premises and multiple cloud providers. It is also possible to extend its functionalities with custom tools, besides making use of a wealth of open source, community-led solutions to ease setup and deployment.

Getting Started with a Cluster on AWS EC2

Although it would be possible to set up a cluster by creating EC2 instances and installing all Kubernetes components on them, this could be quite error-prone and time-consuming. Many tools are available to start deploying a Kubernetes cluster on AWS, in particular:

- Kubernetes Operations (kops) - This is a production grade tool used to install, upgrade and manage Kubernetes on AWS. It has support for different operating systems like Ubuntu, Debian, CentOS and RHEL. This tool has the ability to generate Terraform templates and support custom Kubernetes add-ons.

- Tectonic Installer - This tool was developed by CoreOS to facilitate deployment of secure and highly available Kubernetes clusters on different infrastructure such as AWS, Azure, OpenStack, Google Cloud, and also bare metal. CoreOS is the base operating system for the nodes in a Kubernetes cluster installed by this tool.

- kube-aws - This is a tool by Kubernetes Incubator which can create, update and destroy highly available Kubernetes clusters on AWS backed by multi-AZ deployment. This deployment tool is powered by various AWS services including CloudFormation, Key Management Service, Auto Scaling, Spot Fleet, EC2, ELB, S3, etc and an existing VPC can be used for the deployment.

Deploying Kubernetes on AWS Using Kops

Kops is a production grade tool used to install, upgrade, and operate highly available Kubernetes clusters on AWS and other cloud platforms using the command line. Kops is capable of generating Terraform templates with support for multiple CNI networking plugins and custom Kubernetes add-ons.

Installing a Kubernetes Cluster on AWS

Before proceeding, make sure to have installed kubectl , kops , and AWS cli tools.

Configure AWS Client with Access Credentials

Make sure AWS IAM user has the following permissions for kops to function properly:

- AmazonEC2FullAccess
- AmazonRoute53FullAccess
- AmazonS3FullAccess
- IAMFullAccess
- AmazonVPCFullAccess
- Configure AWS cli with this user's credentials by running:
- # aws configure
- Create S3 Bucket for Cluster State Storage
- Create a dedicated S3 bucket which will be used by kops to store the state representing the cluster. We'll name this bucket my-cluster-state :
- # aws s3api create-bucket --bucket my-cluster-state
- Make sure to activate bucket versioning to be able to later recover or revert to a previous state:
- # aws s3api put-bucket-versioning --bucket my-cluster-state --versioning-configuration Status=Enabled

DNS Setup

On the DNS side, you can go with either public or private DNS. For public DNS, a valid top-level domain or subdomain is required to create the cluster. DNS is required by worker nodes to discover the master and by the master to discover all the etcd servers. For a domain whose registrar is not AWS, create a Route 53 hosted zone on AWS and change nameserver records on your registrar accordingly.

In this example we'll be using a simple, private DNS to create a gossip-based cluster . The only requirement to set this up is for our cluster name to end with k8s.local .

Creating the Kubernetes Cluster

Note that all kops commands below that include --yes option can be run first without it to just show which changes would take place (for example, which AWS resources will get created or destroyed when running the command with --yes option).

The following command will create a 1 master (an m3.medium instance) and 2 nodes (two t2.medium instances) cluster in us-west-2a availability zone:

kops create cluster \ --name my-cluster.k8s.local \ --zones us-west-2a \ --dns private \ --master-size=m3.medium \ --master-count=1 \ --node-size=t2.medium \ --node-count=2 \ --state s3://my-cluster-state \ --yes

Some of the command options in the above example have default values: --master-size , --master-count , --node-size , and --node-count . We've used the default values so the end result would be the same if we hadn't specified those options. Also note that kops will create one master node in each availability zone specified, so this option: --zones us-west-2a,us-west-2b would result in 2 master nodes, one in each of the two zones (even if --master-count was not specified in the command line).

Note that cluster creation may take a while as instances must boot, download the standard Kubernetes components and reach a "ready" state. Kops provides a command to check the state of the cluster and check it's ready:

kops validate cluster --state=s3://my-cluster-state Using cluster from kubectl context: my-cluster.k8s.local Validating cluster my-cluster.k8s.local INSTANCE GROUPS NAME ROLE MACHINETYPE MIN MAX SUBNETS master-us-west-2a Master m3.medium 1 1 us-west-2a nodes Node t2.medium 2 2 us-west-2a NODE STATUS NAME ROLE READY ip-172-20-32-203.us-west-2.compute.internal node True ip-172-20-36-109.us-west-2.compute.internal node True ip-172-20-61-137.us-west-2.compute.internal master True Your cluster my-cluster.k8s.local is ready

If you want to make some changes to the cluster, do so by running:
kops edit cluster my-cluster.k8s.local # kops update cluster my-cluster.k8s.local --yes

Upgrading the Cluster to a Later Kubernetes Release

Kops can upgrade an existing cluster (master and nodes) to the latest recommended release of Kubernetes without having to specify the exact version. Kops supports rolling cluster upgrades where the master and worker nodes are upgraded one by one.

1. Update Kubernetes
kops upgrade cluster \ --name $NAME \ --state s3://my-cluster-state \ --yes

2. Update the state store to match the cluster state.
kops update cluster \ --name my-cluster.k8s.local \ --state s3://my-cluster-state \ --yes

3. Perform the rolling update.
kops rolling-update cluster \ --name my-cluster.k8s.local \ --state s3://my-cluster-state \ --yes

This will perform updates on all instances in the cluster, first master and then workers.

Delete the Cluster

To destroy an existing cluster that we used for experimenting or trials for example, we can run:
kops delete cluster my-cluster.k8s.local \ --state=s3://my-cluster-state \ --yes

Using Kubernetes EKS Managed Service

Amazon Elastic Container Service for Kubernetes (EKS) is a fully managed service that takes care of all the cluster setup and creation, ensuring multi-AZ support on all clusters and automatic replacement of unhealthy instances (master or worker nodes). It also patches and upgrades clusters to the latest recommended Kubernetes release without requiring any intervention.

While EKS provides similar levels of integration with other Amazon services as ECS, it relies on Kubernetes open orchestration model instead of an AWS specific model. This increases the portability of clusters deployed on EKS to other cloud providers. The key contention for such a migration would be the level of coupling with native AWS services, but at least the orchestration side would be easier.

By default clusters in EKS consist of 3 masters spread across 3 different availability zones to protect against the failure of a single AWS availability zone:

Worker nodes are launched on the AWS user's own EC2 instances, thus not shared with other tenants. In order to use tools such as kubectl , access to master instances must be set up via IAM authenticated public endpoints or through AWS PrivateLink . With AWS PrivateLink, masters appear as an elastic network interface with private IP addresses in the Amazon VPC. This allows to the masters and the EKS service directly from the Amazon VPC, without using public IP addresses or requiring the traffic to traverse the internet.

Amazon EKS also integrates tightly with other AWS services such as ELB for load balancing, or AWS CloudTrail for logging.

Standing up a new Kubernetes cluster with EKS can be done simply using the AWS Management Console. After getting access to the cluster, containerized applications can be scheduled in the new cluster in the same fashion as with any other Kubernetes installation:

Launching Kubernetes on EC2 Using Rancher

Rancher is a complete container management platform that eases deployment of Kubernetes and containers. Rancher natively supports Kubernetes and allows users to control its features through a simple UI, including updates to the latest stable release. It integrates with LDAP, AD, and GitHub for authentication. Rancher also provides an application catalog with over 90 popular Docker applications .
Setting Up Rancher in AWS

Rancher (the application) runs on RancherOS, which is available as an Amazon Machine Image (AMI), and thus can be deployed on any EC2 instance.

Create RancherOS Instance on EC2

After installing and configuring AWS CLI tool, proceed to create an EC2 instance using RancherOS AMI. Check RancherOS documentation for AMI ids for each region. For example this command:

```
$ aws ec2 run-instances --image-id ami-12db887d --count 1 --instance-
type t2.micro --key-name my-key-pair --security-groups my-sg
```

will create one new t2.micro EC2 instance with RancherOS on ap-south-1 AWS region. Make sure to use the correct key name and security group. Also make sure the security group enables traffic to TCP port 8080 to the new instance.

Start Rancher Server

When the new instance is ready, just connect using ssh and start the Rancher server:

```
$ sudo docker run --name rancher-server -d --restart=unless-stopped \
  -p 8080:8080 rancher/server:stable
```

This might take a few minutes. Once done, the UI can be accessed on port 8080 of the EC2 instance . Since by default anyone can access Rancher's UI and API, it is recommended to set up access control.
Creating a Kubernetes cluster via Rancher in AWS

Configure Kubernetes environment template

An environment in Rancher is a logical entity for sharing deployments and resources with different sets of users. Environments are created from templates. Rancher's application catalogue already includes templates for Kubernetes that can be selected and modified to configure, among other: disabling add-ons (Rancher installs by default: Helm ,

Dashboard and SkyDNS), enabling backups , and selecting the cloud provider for managing load balancers, nodes and networking routes.

Create the Kubernetes Cluster (environment)

Adding a Kubernetes environment is just a matter of selecting the adequately configured template for our use case and inputting the cluster name. If access control is turned on, we can add members and select their membership role . Anyone added to the membership list would have access to the environment.

Add Hosts to Kubernetes Cluster

We need to add at least one host to the newly created Kubernetes environment. In this case, the hosts will be previously created AWS EC2 instances.

Once the first host has been added, Rancher will automatically start the deployment of the infrastructure (master) including Kubernetes services (i.e. kubelet, etcd, kube-proxy, etc). Hosts that will be used as Kubernetes nodes will require TCP ports 10250 and 10255 to be open for kubectl. Make sure to review the full list of Rancher requirements for the hosts .

It might take a few minutes for the Kubernetes cluster setup/update to complete, after adding hosts to Kubernetes environment:

Deploying Applications in the Kubernetes Cluster

Once the cluster is ready containerized applications can be deployed using either the Rancher application catalog or kubectl. kubectl needs to be configured via the Rancher UI in order for deployment information to become visible in Rancher's dashboards.

Scheduling Kubernetes Resources on AWS Using Terraform

Terraform is an infrastructure-as-code tool used for building, changing, and versioning infrastructure safely and efficiently. It can be used to deploy containerized applications into an properly configured Kubernetes cluster running in AWS.

Terraform uses its own configuration language and by default looks for resource specifications in the same directory where the terraform commands are being executed.
Specifying Kubernetes as Provider

Terraform needs to be informed of the Kubernetes cluster configuration. For example this Terraform configuration file (extension .tf):
provider "kubernetes" { host = "https://104.196.242.174" username = "my-user" password = "my-password" client_certificate = "${file("~/.kube/client-cert.pem")}" client_key = "${file("~/.kube/client-key.pem")}" cluster_ca_certificate = "${file("~/.kube/cluster-ca-cert.pem")}" }

tells Terraform that the Kubernetes master is located at the host IP address and provides the AWS credentials and certificates to ssh to it. We can then install the Terraform plugin for Kubernetes provider by running the command:
terraform init
Specifying and Deploying Pods and Services

Kubernetes resources like pods and services can be created using Terraform's configuration language (which then gets translated transparently by Terraform to actual Kubernetes specifications). For example to create a single (nginx) pod and a service selecting this pod:
resource "kubernetes_pod" "nginx" { metadata { name = "nginx-example" labels { App = "nginx" } } spec { container { image = "nginx:1.7.8" name = "example" port { container_port = 80 } } } } resource "kubernetes_service" "nginx" { metadata { name = "nginx-example" } spec { selector { App = "${kubernetes_pod.nginx.metadata.0.labels.App}" } port { port = 80 target_port = 80 } type = "LoadBalancer" } }

Running the terraform plan command will display the list of actions (resources to destroy, change or create) that Terraform will perform based on the above configuration:
+ kubernetes_pod.nginx + kubernetes_service.nginx Plan: 2 to add, 0 to change, 0 to destroy.

Note that the whole configuration of both the pod and service are displayed, but were omitted here for brevity.

Finally, to actually deploy the pod and service, the terraform apply command must be executed. This will create resources via the API in the right order, supplying any defaults as necessary and waiting for resources to finish provisioning to the point when it can either present useful attributes or a failure (with reason) to the user.

Other Options for Deploying Kubernetes in the Cloud

Besides the Kubernetes deployment options already covered, there are other tools that can be used to deploy Kubernetes on public clouds like AWS. Each tool has its unique features and building blocks:

- Heptio - Heptio provides a solution based on CloudFormation and kubeadm to deploy Kubernetes on AWS, and supports multi-AZ. Heptio is suitable for users already familiar with CloudFormation AWS orchestration tool.

- Kismatic Enterprise Toolkit (KET) - KET is a collection of tools with sensible defaults which are production-ready to create enterprise-tuned clusters of Kubernetes. The goal with this toolkit is to make it easy for organizations to install and manage their Kubernetes infrastructure and clusters.

- kubeadm - The kubeadm project is focused on a solution to build a simple cluster on AWS using Terraform. It is an adequate tool for tests and proof-of-concepts only as it doesn't support multi-AZ and other advanced features.

- OpenShift - This is a Red Hat platform-as-a-service product for container-based deployment and management of software. There is an open source version called OpenShift Origin which adds developer and operations-centric tools on top of Kubernetes to enable rapid application development, easy deployment and scaling, and long-term lifecycle maintenance for small and large teams.

- Stackpoint - This is a web based solution that provides a user friendly platform to provision Kubernetes on various cloud providers such as AWS, Google Cloud Platform, Microsoft Azure and Digital Ocean. This is a good tool for those using more than one cloud provider and would like a single place for managing their multi-cloud Kubernetes deployments.

- Tack - This is a terraform module that can be used to create Kubernetes clusters which run on any version of CoreOS on AWS. Supports multi-AZ deployments of worker nodes that are able to auto-scale.

- Tectonic - Tectonic enables an automated installation of Kubernetes with the goals of being secure by default, quick and easy to install clusters, highly available, modular and customizable. It also focuses on portability (runs on any operating system), and flexibility of deployment to multiple cloud providers such as AWS, Google Cloud Platform, or Microsoft Azur.

BENEFITS OF KUBERNETES

Kubernetes is an open source orchestrator for deploying and managing containerized applications at scale. Kubernetes was originally developed by Google, based on their learnings from Borg and Omega Projects, which Google uses to deploy and scale their internal applications (e.g: GMail, YouTube etc).

So what does Kubernetes do? Well to put it simply, it provides tools necessary to build and deploy reliable, scalable distributed applications. To elaborate further, in modern architectures, huge number of services are delivered over the network via APIs. These are delivered via distribution systems running on multiple servers and configurations in various locations all coordinating their actions via network communication. Gone are the days we used to simply deploy an application in one VM and used to point a DNS to it. Load is balanced and horizontal scalability is achieved by making systems distributed like these. We are using these exposed APIs on a daily basis, all around the globe, these systems should be highly reliable and available, ie; they cannot fail and should not have any downtime. Since these services are accessed from all around the world, they should be scalable as well, without a radical redesign of the existing system. Kubernetes provides relevant services to achieve all of this for your containerized application.

Let's discuss the major benefits of using containers and a container orchestration platform like Kubernetes.

Velocity

The speed at which you constantly update your application and deploy it's new features to the users. Back in the day, to update a software or when pushing a new deployment, there was a lot of a downtime and was usually done in the midnight or over the weekend where the user traffic was at a minimum. However, you should note that when continuously deploying new features with downtime does not increase velocity. The goal is it update the application without a downtime as users expect a constant uptime. Therefore velocity is measure through the number of features you could ship per hour while maintaining a highly available service.

The core concepts of Kubernetes which enables high velocity are immutability, declarative configuration and self healing systems which are discussed below.

Immutability

Containers and Kubernetes encourage developers to build distributed systems that adhere to the principles of immutable infrastructure. In immutable infrastructure an artifact created, will not be changed upon user modifications.

Traditional way of doing things with mutable infrastructure was, allowing changes to happen on top of existing objects as incremental updates. Therefore, the current state of the infrastructure cannot be represented as one single artifact, but rather an accumulation of incremental updates and changes of that artifact.

When it comes to updating an application in traditional way, what you would do is either log into a VM or existing container and download the latest software binaries of your application, kill the server and restart it. If something goes wrong, with multiple updates, you don't have any record of how many updates you deployed and at which point the errors started to occur.

In immutable infrastructure, if you want to update your application, you simply build a new container image with a new tag, and you deploy it, killing the old container with the old image version. This way, you always have an artifact record of what you did and if there was an error in your new image, you could easily rollback to the previous image.

Declarative Configuration

Everything in kubernetes is a declarative configuration object that represents the desired state of the system. This is an alternative to the traditional imperative configuration, where the state of system is defined by the execution of a series of instructions rather than a declaration of desired state of the system.

An example to explain the above simply is, consider a task of running 3 replicas of a piece of software. With imperative configuration, it would be, "run A, run B, run C" whereas with declarative configuration, it would simply be, "replicas = 3"

Declarative configuration enables the user to describe exactly what state the system should be in and is far less error prone. Traditional tools of development such as source control, unit tests etc can be used with declarative configurations in ways that are impossible with imperative configurations. This makes rollbacks fairly easy for kubernetes which is impossible with imperative configurations. Imperative systems basically describe how to get from point A to B, but rarely include reverse instructions to get you back.

Self Healing Systems

When kubernetes receive a desired state configuration, it does not simply take actions to make the current state match the desired state at a single time, but it will continuously take actions to ensure it stays that way as time passes by.

Example for this is, if you assert a desired state of 3 replicas of a certain application, kubernetes would not only create 3 replicas, but it will continuously ensure that there are exactly 3 replicas. If you manually destroy one, kubernetes will bring one back up to match the desired state.

Scaling Services

As the product grows, you have to scale both your software and teams working on it. Kubernetes achieves scalability by favoring decoupled architectures.

Decoupling

In a decoupled architecture, each component is separated from other components by defined APIs and service load balancers. APIs provide a buffer between implementer and consumer, and load balancers provide a buffer between running instances of each service. Decoupling components via load balancers makes it easier to scale the programs that make up your service, because increasing the size of the program can be done without adjusting or reconfiguring any of the other layers of your service.

Scaling Applications and Clusters

Scaling is fairly easy due to the immutable, declarative nature of kubernetes which was explained earlier. Because the containers are immutable, the number of replicas is simply a number in the declarative config which could be changed whenever required. Of course you can set up auto scaling as well with kubernetes which will take care of everything for you.

However, with autoscaling, it assumes that there are enough resources available. If not, you will have to scale up the cluster itself. Kubernetes makes this task easier as well because every machine in the cluster is identical to every other machine and the applications themselves are decoupled from the machine by containers, adding additional resources is simply a matter of creating a new machine with required binaries using a pre-baked image and joining it to the new cluster.
Building decoupled microservice architectures

When building microservice architectures, multiple teams work on a single service each which would be consumed by other teams for their service implementation. The aggregation of all of these services ultimately provides the implementation of overall product's surface area.

Kubernetes provides numerous abstractions and APIs to enable this.

- Pods, or groups of containers can group together container images developed by different teams into a single deployable unit.
- Kubernetes services provide load balancing, naming and discovery to isolate one microservice from another.
- Namespaces provide isolation and access control so that each microservice can control the degree to which other services interact with it.

This means that decoupling the application container image and machine allows different microservices to colocate on the same machine without interfering the other, reducing the overhead and the cost of microservice architectures.

The health checking and rollout features of Kubernetes guarantee a consistent approach to application rollout and reliability as well.

Separation of Concerns

To explain this simply, The application developer relies on the SLA (Service level Agreement) delivered by the container orchestration API, without worrying about how it is achieved and likewise, the orchestration API reliability engineer focuses on delivering the orchestration API's SLA without worrying about the applications that run on top of it.

This separation of concerns or decoupling means that a small team running a Kubernetes cluster can be responsible for supporting thousands of teams running their applications within that cluster.

Abstraction of Infrastructure

Kubernetes separates developers from specific machines. In context of the cloud, this enables a high degree of portability since developers are consuming a higher level API that is implemented in terms of the specific cloud infrastructure APIs.

This allows developers to transfer their applications between environments which is a matter of sending the declarative configuration to the new cluster. Kubernetes has a number of plugins that can abstract you from a particular cloud. For example, kubernetes knows how to create load balancers on all major public clouds as well as several different private and physical infrastructures.

Efficiency

In Kubernetes, applications can be colocated on the same machines without impacting each other. This means that tasks from multiple users can be packed tightly onto fewer machines. This in turn provides greater efficiency and also reduces the cost on hardware as less machines are used.

Conclusion

Kubernetes was built to radically change the way applications are built and deployed in the cloud as it was designed to give developers more velocity, efficiency and agility.

THE BENEFITS AND BUSINESS VALUE OF KUBERNETES

Container technology caught the public's attention with the introduction of Docker in 2013. The efficiency and cost benefits containerisation can offer quickly made it one of the hottest topics in cloud computing. Shortly after Dockers' release, there has been a flood of new container management platforms, aiming to reduce the complexity of managing containerised applications. One of these platforms, the open source project Kubernetes, is by now the de facto standard for container management.

To understand the power of Kubernetes, you should have some basic knowledge about containers. In our previous blog posts we explained the basics of container technology, talked about the benefits of containers, turned surveys about container adoption into a Docker infographic and more. In case you missed it, let's start with a short reminder of what containers actually are.

What are containers and where does Kubernetes fit in?

"A container image is a lightweight, stand-alone, executable package of a piece of software that includes everything needed to run it: code, runtime, system tools, system libraries, settings….(..)…Containers isolate software from its surroundings, for example differences between development and staging environments and help reduce conflicts between teams running different software on the same infrastructure."

In practice, containers enable you to make highly efficient use of the underlying infrastructure and develop and deploy applications more rapidly – a killer combination of benefits. It's no wonder start-ups, SME as well as enterprises are adopting container technology at an explosive rate. 451 Research predicts more than 250% growth in the market from 2016 to 2020.

Deploying a container is relatively simple, shortly after Dockers' release, lots of software-companies started using the technology in their software development and test process. But when it comes to actually running containers in production, you can end up with dozens – or even millions when using micro-services – of containers over time. All these containers need to be deployed, managed and connected to the outside world including scheduling, load balancing and distribution. Imagine you doing this manually; You would need an entire dev or ops army to accomplish this. This is where container orchestration (a.k.a. container management) i.e. Kubernetes comes to the rescue.

What is Kubernetes

Kubernetes, is a container management system, was originally created at Google. In 2015, Google released Kubernetes as an open-source project. Shortly after that Kubernetes was donated to the Cloud Native Computing Foundation (CNCF). The CNCF, initialised by Google in cooperation with the Linux Foundation, aims to promote container technology.

What does Kubernetes actually do?

In short, Kubernetes enables you to make the potential of container technology an operational reality by automating and simplifying your daily container workflow. Kubernetes automates deploying, scaling and managing containerised applications on a group (cluster) of (bare metal or virtual) servers. Kubernetes also lets you automatically handle networking, storage, logs, alerting, etc. for all your containers. To avoid going into 'tech-mode', we will try to explain Kubernetes' strengths, main features and benefits in plain English, without going into too much detail. If you are interested in diving deeper into what Kubernetes is, the technology of Kubernetes, the Kubernetes architecture and components, we can refer you to the official Kubernetes documentation.

The business value of adopting containerisation and deploying Kubernetes

Enterprises, SME's as well as start-ups are adopting container technology and Kubernetes with breathtaking speed. If your company is interested in embracing this technology, it's important to keep in mind you shouldn't turn to container technology or Kubernetes simply because 'everyone' seems to do so. Adopting containerisation and Kubernetes (or any other container management tool) as a stand-alone goal is the wrong way to look at it, instead the implementation should support your business, operational and strategic goals. In this blog post we will try to translate the idea behind container technology and the main features of Kubernetes into business value.

Benefits and advantages of containerisation

Before we dive into the benefits Kubernetes brings to the table, we'll explore the main benefits of Docker:

- **Reducing resource costs:**

Let's kick off with an advantage that every company will appeal to: reducing expenses. Containers are isolated 'packages', that include everything the application needs to properly run. Multiple containers can share the same OS and network connection. This is much more efficient when it comes to resource utilisation than creating a virtual machine with its own OS for each application. Containers are lightweight by design and take up fewer resources, enabling you to save on hardware and data centre costs.

- **Ease-of-use and portability:**

The isolation containers offer enables you to run your software consistently across environments. On your laptop, on any public cloud, private cloud, or even bare metal. Containers can also be copied to development, test, integration and live environments quickly and reliably. This greatly simplifies and speeds up the software development and release process, resulting in a faster time-to-market. This advantage offers more opportunities that at first sight may not be so obvious. Think for example of your overall business goal to improve your customer relations. It probably won't be the first thing that comes to mind, but containerisation gives you the ability to respond quickly to customer requests for bug fixes or new features: something your customers will greatly appreciate.

- **Scalability and modularity:**

Since containers are lightweight by design, they can be created within seconds. This enables you to scale instantly, helping you for example to react to unexpected website traffic load seamlessly. Containers also make it really easy to break down your application into individual components with their own function. You might want to have your application in one container and your database running in another container. Docker lets you link these containers together to create your application, making it easy to update or scale the components independently. This advantage shines even more when used in combination with a micro services architecture where an application is built out of loosely coupled services that communicate through simple API's.

Benefits and advantages of using Kubernetes

There are a lot of options when it comes to container management, both open source and commercial. Kubernetes, however, is the most widely used solution and has surged in popularity in the past several years.
Let's find out why:
The case for Kubernetes v.s. other container management systems

- **Impressive heritage:**

Kubernetes has a very mature and proven underlying architecture. Its design is built on over 10 years of operational experience of the Google engineers who helped build and maintain the largest container platform in the world.

- **Outstanding community and industry support:**

Kubernetes' broad adoption, growth, support and popularity stands out among all other container orchestration solutions. The project gained a very large active user and developer open source community, as well as the support of global enterprises, IT market leaders and major cloud providers.

- **Rich feature set and application support:**

Kubernetes has a very rich feature set compared to other container management systems. It supports a wide spectrum of workloads, programming languages and frameworks, enabling stateless, stateful, and data-processing workloads. and making Kubernetes flexible enough to meet the needs of a wide range of users and use cases.

- **Ongoing development:**

Soon after its first release, Kubernetes gained a very large and active community. With about 2000 Github contributors at the moment, varying from engineers working at fortune 500 companies to individual developers and engineers, new features are being released constantly. The large and diverse user community also steps in to answer questions and foster collaboration.

Kubernetes' main features and benefits

Now that we've covered why Kubernetes is winning the container orchestration war, let's have a look at the features Kubernetes has to offer. To understand the Kubernetes features, it's good to know that applications deployed in Kubernetes are composed of multiple containers grouped as pods. Pods are co-located containers that share resources like filesystems, kernel namespaces and an IP adress. We have been working with Kubernetes for two years now, and it has became one of our favourite tools to build the versatile, tailored IT solutions our customers rely on us for. The full feature set Kubernetes offers is much too large to cover in this blog post, but we'll discuss the main benefits and features.

- **It's portable and 100% open source:**

Kubernetes can practically be deployed on any infrastructure. Run your containers in one or more public cloud environments, on your dedicated virtual machines or on bare metal. You can use the same orchestration tool for all your different environments. Kubernetes' compatibility across several platforms avoids infrastructure and cloud provider lock-in and makes a multi-cloud strategy and setup not only possible, but highly usable and flexible as well. The project is 100% open source, providing you with even more flexibility. Should you decide to hire external experts to help you implement and maintain your Kubernetes solution, you can easily switch providers if you are unsatisfied with their quality of service (provided you don't use a specific commercial platform built upon Kubernetes).

- **Workload Scalability**

Kubernetes is known to be efficient in its use of infrastructure resources and offers several useful features for scaling purposes:

- Horizontal infrastructure scaling: Kubernetes operates at the individual server level to implement horizontal scaling. New servers can be added or removed easily.
- Auto-scaling: With auto-scaling you can automatically change the number of running containers, based on CPU utilisation or other application-provided metrics.
- Manual scaling: You can manually scale the number of running containers through a command or the interface.
- Replication controller: The Replication controller makes sure your cluster has a specified number of equivalent pods (a group of containers) running. If there are too many pods, the Replication Controller terminates the extra pods. If there are too few, it starts more pods.

- **High Availability**

Kubernetes is designed to tackle the availability of both applications and infrastructure, making it indispensable when deploying containers in production:

- Health checks and self-healing: Kubernetes guards your containerised application against failures by constantly checking the health of nodes and containers. Kubernetes also offers self-healing and auto-replacement: if a container or pod crashes due to an error, Kubernetes has got you covered.
- Traffic routing and load balancing: traffics routing sends requests to the appropriate containers. Kubernetes also comes in with built-in load balancers to distribute your load across multiple pods, enabling you to (re)balance resources

quickly in order to respond to outages, peak or incidental traffic and batch processing. It's also possible to use external load balancers.

- **Designed for deployment**

One of the main benefits of containersation is the ability to speed up the process of building, testing, and releasing software. Kubernetes is designed for deployment, and offers several useful features:
- Automated rollouts and rollbacks: Want to roll-out a new version of your app or update its configuration? Kubernetes will handle it for you without downtime, while monitoring the containers' health during the roll-out. In case of failure, it automatically rolls back.
- Canary Deployments: Canary deployments enable you to test the new deployment in production in parallel with the previous version, before scaling up the new deployment and simultaneously scaling down the previous deployment.
- Programming languages and frameworks support: Kubernetes support a wide spectrum of programming languages and frameworks like Java, Go, .Net, etc. Kubernetes also has a lot of support from the development community, who maintain additional programming languages and frameworks. If an application can run in a container, it should run well on Kubernetes.

And more
Yes, there is more. Kubernetes offers DNS management, resource monitoring, logging and storage orchestration (automatically mount the

necessary storage system, be it local storage, or public cloud provider storage). Kubernetes also offers features to address security, for example by making sure sensitive information like passwords or ssh keys, are stored securely in Kubernetes secrets. Both the secrets and the configuration of applications are deployed and updated without having to reconstruct the image or expose confidential information. New features are being released constantly, and can be found on the Kubernetes GitHub page.

Kubernetes solutions for enterprises:

Let's say you have done your research, and you are sure you want to use Kubernetes as your container management system. What are your options?

Do it yourself (perhaps with a little help)

It's possible to build your own Kubernetes cluster from scratch, but as mentioned above, successfully setting up and maintaining a secure, highly available Kubernetes cluster is a lot of work. The process is complex and time-consuming. There are lots of companies out there that can provide you with Kubernetes consulting, training or workshops to help you get on the right track. However, when using Kubernetes in production, you will still need a team of at least 3 employees with expensive Kubernetes skills available at all times, in case anything goes wrong. In most cases and for most organisations, this just isn't feasible.

Managed Kubernetes platforms (SaaS-solutions)

There is no shortage of commercial offerings based upon Kubernetes. New solutions are popping up every day. Most of these solutions are offerings from companies that build their own product around Kubernetes. The drawback of many of these Kubernetes platforms is that they are designed to simplify the use of Kubernetes management, and focus primarily on providing a simplified user interface (UI), instead of addressing the fundamental challenges of working with containerised applications and creating a production-ready environment. There are some nice options out there, but keep in mind that most of them limit the degree of customisation and lock you in to one specific product.

Fully Managed Kubernetes (IT outsourcing)

As a third option, you can hire Kubernetes specialists to implement and/or maintain your Kubernetes infrastructure, without the use of any commercial tools. Some providers offer consulting and implementation to help you get on the right track. Other service providers also offer day-to-day management and support. This is similar to traditional managed services and IT outsourcing.

The pace of Kubernetes adoption is creating a high demand for specialists that provide extended support and ongoing cluster operation services. This is why the Cloud Native Computing Foundation (CNCF) launched the Kubernetes Certified Service Provider Program. The KCSP program is a pre-qualified tier of vetted service providers who have extensive experience helping enterprises successfully adopt Kubernetes. We at Kumina are committed to being one of these specialists and are proud to say we are a Certified Kubernetes Service Partner.

HOW TO DEVELOP KUBERNETES-FRIENDLY CONTAINERISED APPLICATIONS

There's a lot out there that describes how to setup Kubernetes and how to make your container run on Kubernetes, but fairly little in regard to how you should be *developing* for Kubernetes. I hope to provide you with some guidance for this! Which is a bit ironic, as I'm actually not a developer but a sysadmin. So keep in mind that you're free to write better code than mine, the code I provide here is for educational purposes only.

This installment of the post will just set up the basics. We'll end up with a local "cluster" (using minikube) and even smaller application that we can run on it and examine. Nothing fancy, just settings things up for the next post in which we'll start tackling some of the problems we'll encounter.

We would be writing the code in Python 3, but even if you're not proficient with Python 3, I hope the code is simple enough that you can follow along in your own prefered language. I'll assume you're using Python 3.5 or higher (I've only tested my code on Python 3.5.3 on Linux).

A simple application

Let's start with a simple example application, my_webserver.py:

```python
import http.server

class MyWebpage(http.server.BaseHTTPRequestHandler):
    def do_GET(s):
        s.send_response(200)
        s.send_header('Content-Type', 'text/html')
        s.end_headers()
        s.wfile.write(b'''
<!DOCTYPE html>
<html>
  <head>
    <title>Hello!</title>
  </head>
  <body>
    <p>This is a demo page!</p>
  </body>
</html>''')

if __name__ == '__main__':
    httpd = http.server.HTTPServer(('127.0.0.1', 8080), MyWebpage)
    httpd.serve_forever()
```

When you run this script with python3 my_webserver.py, it will open port 8080 on your lo device. You can check if it works when you open another terminal and do:

```
$ echo "GET / HTTP/1.0" | nc localhost 8080
HTTP/1.0 200 OK
Server: BaseHTTP/0.6 Python/3.5.2
Date: Mon, 02 Oct 2017 12:30:09 GMT
Content-Type: text/html


<!DOCTYPE html>
<html>
  <head>
    <title>Hello!</title>
  </head>
  <body>
    <p>This is a demo page!</p>
  </body>
</html>
```

You can of course also use a browser to visithttp://127.0.0.1:8080, which will show you a simple page with a single line on it.

This script is but a simple HTTP server, as it allows me to show you what problems you can encounter and how to deal with them. If you want to do something more elaborate, I would recommend using a framework of some sort, like Django or Flask. But for this series of post, a simple HTTP server will suffice.

Setting up Kubernetes

Next, we need to run this on Kubernetes. As this is just a demonstration, I'm going to use minikube to show how this would work on Kubernetes.

I'm using version 0.22.2, but it should work on later versions as well. Start out with starting your cluster:

```
$ minikube start
Starting local Kubernetes v1.7.5 cluster...
Starting VM...
Getting VM IP address...
Moving files into cluster...
Setting up certs...
Connecting to cluster...
Setting up kubeconfig...
Starting cluster components...
Kubectl is now configured to use the cluster.
$ kubectl config use-context minikube
Context "minikube" modified.
$ eval $(minikube docker-env)
$
```

So, we now have a local Kubernetes running inide a VM, we've setup kubectl to actually use it by default (which saves us from typing --context minikube for each kubectl invocation).

Next, we're going to create a simple Docker image for our application inside the minikube VM (so we do not have to publish it anywhere online).

Packaging our application

To do so, we're going to create a file called Dockerfile. This is the content:

```
FROM python:alpine3.6
WORKDIR /usr/src/app
COPY my_webserver.py ./
CMD ["python", "./my_webserver.py"]
```

For those unfamiliar with Dockerfiles, the first line makes sure we use the upstream python:alpine3.6 as our base. This is a small image available from the Docker hub that can easily be modified for running Python apps. Most languages (NodeJS, Ruby, Java, etc.) have these kind of base images available on Docker hub, you can search for them here (don't worry about creating an account, you don't need it to just use the images). As Docker hub is the default repository, you do not need to add a hostname in that line.

The next line sets the working directory, in this case essentiatly doing a cd /usr/src/appto make sure all following commands are run from that directory. Than we copy our little my_webserver.pyto that local directory (and thus creating /usr/src/app/my_webserver.py within the image). Lastly, we tell how the application can be started. The python command is part of the image and because we've set a working directory, we can just use ./my_webserver.py as the location of our script.

We then build our own custom image, based on the python:alpine3.6 image, like so:

$ docker build -t my_webserver:0.1 .

This command will build an image using the Dockerfile in this directory and name it my_webserver:0.1. Keep in mind here that we're using the Docker engine running within the minikube VM, as we ran the eval command for that after starting minikube. The image will therefore be built inside the VM and can be accessed by Kubernetes directly. That's helpful, as it means we do not need a registry available to be able to download the image.
Running our application on Kubernetes

Let's try starting the image immediately:

kubectl run mywebserver --image=my_webserver:0.1 --image-pull-policy=Never --restart=Never

The options are important. We name our Pod mywebserver (an underscore is illegal in the name, so we cannot name it my_webserver). Next we tell Kubernetes to use the image that we just built, my_webserver:0.1. If we used an actual registry, we could leave the :0.1 part out of there, as the image will automatically be tagged as latest as well and that's what Kubernetes (or rather, Docker) will start if you do not provide your own version tag. But we're not using a registry, so we have to be a bit more explicit. That's fine though, being explicit with regards to the image version tag is a good thing, as it will allow you to roll back in case of problems.

The next option instructs Kubernetes to never try to download the image. That's what we want, as we have the images locally and we're not pushing them to Docker hub (which is the default server the Docker engine will try to download from if you do not provide a server name) or another registry for that matter. Lastly, we tell Kubernetes we do not want this Pod to automatically restart.

That restart option is important, because if we do not set it, Kubernetes will create a Deployment instead! Deployments are great, but not what we currently want to use. A third option would be to provide the --restart=OnFailure option , which would create a Job. Jobs are used for batch processing and have a slightly different use compared to Pods. We want a Pod, however, so we tell Kubernetes to Never restart. Both Deployments and Jobs might be a subject for another blog series, if you like. Let me know if you'd be interested in something like that!
Kubernetes networking

You now have your first home-made Pod running, which is great! But how to test that it works correctly? It's running inside a VM, so we need to punch a hole through to there. The trouble is, this is pretty hard, as we've configured our code to listen on 127.0.0.1! So we need to change that first. Start with stopping the Pod:

```
$ kubectl delete pod mywebserver
$ kubectl get pods
NAME          READY   STATUS        RESTARTS   AGE
mywebserver   1/1     Terminating   0          27s
```

Keep running the kubectl get pods command every second or so until you no longer see the mywebserver Pod in the list. (Why does it take so long? We'll get to that in a future blog in this series! And fix it as well...) Now we change the line before the last line in our my_webserver.py script, change it to:

httpd = http.server.HTTPServer(('0.0.0.0', 8080), MyWebpage)

(So simply change the 127.0.0.1 into 0.0.0.0.)

Now rebuild the image and remember to increase the tag:

```
$ docker build -t my_webserver:0.2 .
Sending build context to Docker daemon  3.584kB
Step 1 : FROM python:alpine3.6
 ---> 1b1ac8f23f73
Step 2 : WORKDIR /usr/src/app
 ---> Using cache
 ---> 5ef4a439346c
Step 3 : COPY my_webserver.py ./
 ---> af79248c42a3
Removing intermediate container 1d06297fe6b5
Step 4 : CMD python ./my_webserver.py
 ---> Running in 72c3032c5ce4
 ---> 02b0933a611f
Removing intermediate container 72c3032c5ce4
Successfully built 02b0933a611f
```

Listening on 0.0.0.0 will make it listen on all IP addresses that are available (to the container once it runs), which is exactly what we want. As a container is used to contain the process, you can expose your application without worrying about security at this time. Security is based on how we expose the application eventually in the production environment. Once you start creating your own applications, just make them listen on all interfaces. And on whatever port you like (for now... We'll do something with that later on as well!).

Let's run our Pod again and this time, let's be a bit more explicit about the port we want to expose:

```
$ kubectl run mywebserver --image=my_webserver:0.2 --image-pull-policy=Never --restart=Never --port 8080
pod "mywebserver" created
```

This by itself doesn't do anything worthwhile, except give a hint for our next step:

```
$ kubectl expose pod mywebserver --type=NodePort
service "mywebserver" exposed
```

Exposing a Pod allows you to actually access it, it creates a Service for that. A Service is an object within Kubernetes that keeps track of how you allow connections to a Pod. Services exist in several types, the simplest one being a ClusterIP. A ClusterIP creates an IP address within a Kubernetes that makes the Pods behind the Service available via an internal-only IP address. You won't be able to connect to there (easily, by default) from outside the Kubernetes network. This is useful for backend services which only need to be accessed from within the cluster itself.

The second type and the one we use, is the NodePort. A NodePort actually creates a ClusterIP automatically, but also makes a connection to the ClusterIP on the port exposed by the Pod when you connect to any host within the cluster network on that specific port. This means that if you have a worker node with IP address 192.168.0.1 running the mywebserver Pod, you would be able to connect to http://192.168.0.1:8080 to access that port on the Pod. You actually have some freedom here, where you can assign different ports as NodePort and exposed port. (We'll touch on that in a later installment of this series.)

The third type, LoadBalancer, only works when you use one of the supported cloud providers (like Google Cloud Engine or Amazon Web Services). It'll talk to the cloud provider's API to provide actual loadbalancing services for the exposed NodePort on all your workers. This does not work on minikube, but it's good to be aware of this. That said, I would prefer that you learn how to use Ingress controllers and Ingress resources instead, as they tend to be more flexible and very much more portable between Kubernetes environments.

There are a few other ones (ExternalName and ExternalIP), which are not used that much in my experience. They require additional external setup to work correctly.

Ok, so we now have our application exposed, how do we connect? Minikube to the rescue, as it has some tools which help make this a bit easier. Try the following:

$ curl $(minikube service mywebserver --url)

Hopefully, you'll see our little HTML page! Minikube can return the correct IP address for the service in a way that you can easily use it to test. Feel free to just run minikube service mywebserver --url to see what it does.

Graceful termination of containers

First, let's start up the cluster again:

```
$ minikube start
Starting local Kubernetes v1.7.5 cluster...
Starting VM...
Getting VM IP address...
Moving files into cluster...
Setting up certs...
Connecting to cluster...
Setting up kubeconfig...
Starting cluster components...
Kubectl is now configured to use the cluster.
$ eval $(minikube docker-env)
```

Don't forget that last command, as you won't have access to the Docker engine within the Minikube VM otherwise.

So, regarding the delay. The delay is caused by Kubernetes wanting to give an application time to shut itself down. The container first gets a SIGTERM signal. If that does not shut it down within 30 seconds, a SIGKILL signal is sent. Our Python-based web server does not respond to this signal by default, which makes shutting it down fairly slow. This hampers your control over the network, as Kubernetes works best when it can shutdown (and start!) a container fairly quick.

Let's do something about that. Luckily, it's pretty easy in Python to catch a signal and actually do something with it. For completeness sake, I'll provide the entire script, including my new changes, here:

```
import http.server
import sys
import threading
import signal

class MyWebpage(http.server.BaseHTTPRequestHandler):
    def do_GET(s):
        s.send_response(200)
        s.send_header('Content-Type', 'text/html')
        s.end_headers()
        s.wfile.write(b'''
<!DOCTYPE html>
<html>
  <head>
    <title>Hello!</title>
  </head>
  <body>
    <p>This is a demo page!</p>
  </body>
</html>''')

if __name__ == '__main__':
    def do_shutdown(signum, frame):
```

> *threading.Thread(target = httpd.shutdown).start()*
> *sys.exit(0)*
>
> *signal.signal(signal.SIGTERM, do_shutdown)*
>
> *httpd = http.server.HTTPServer(('0.0.0.0', 8080), MyWebpage)*
> *httpd.serve_forever()*

So we create a function that actually performs the shutdown in a separate thread. This is an implementation detail of the http.server.HTTPServer (I had to google it myself as well). Then we catch the specific signal and call the function. It's as simple as that.

In a more elaborate application, this is where you can do cleanup stuff, like making sure no new connections are allowed, finishing running queries or logging some things. You want this to be fast, though. If the cleanup phase takes more than 30 seconds, the container will get a SIGKILL and there's no way to catch that one. You can of course tell Kubernetes to wait a bit longer (this is called the grace period, which defaults to the aforementioned 30 seconds), but I would not recommend this unless you have a really, really good reason. It makes your cluster respond a lot slower if it needs to wait on shutdowns for a long time.

Let's use the Dockerfile from the previous session again and build a new image.

> *$ docker build -t my_webserver:0.3 .*
> *Sending build context to Docker daemon 3.584kB*
> *Step 1 : FROM python:alpine3.6*

```
---> 1b1ac8f23f73
Step 2 : WORKDIR /usr/src/app
---> Using cache
---> 5ef4a439346c
Step 3 : COPY my_webserver.py ./
---> f9202dc0c68e
Removing intermediate container 89f4281c0aee
Step 4 : CMD python ./my_webserver.py
---> Running in dd417b54f619
---> 963f5b0c5346
Removing intermediate container dd417b54f619
Successfully built 963f5b0c5346
```

And run it again:

```
$ kubectl run mywebserver --image=my_webserver:0.3 --image-pull-policy=Never --restart=Never --port=8080
pod "mywebserver" created
```

Now delete the Pod again and check how long it takes. We'll use a one-liner for it, as the result is pretty fast (on my machine at least):

```
$ kubectl delete pod mywebserver && kubectl get pods && sleep 1 && kubectl get pods
pod "mywebserver" deleted
NAME          READY   STATUS        RESTARTS   AGE
mywebserver   1/1     Terminating   0          1m
No resources found, use --show-all to see completed objects.
```

As you can see, we now have a Pod that's responsive to being terminated. The main advantage we have with that is that it's now a lot faster to perform a deployment of a new image via rolling-updates.

Another aspect of being able to make fast deployments is the size of the image. I won't reiterate what's already been said about that in depth. Just keep in mind that you want your images as small as possible. A container should not be like a VM or VPS. The idea behind containers is process isolation, so you want the least amount of code in there, just enough to be able to run your applications. At this point in time, using Alpine based images seems to be a very good way to achieve this, but investigate your options. Size does matter, at least in this regard.

Logging

Let's expose the Pod again (if you still have the mywebserver Service set up, you can skip this):

```
$ kubectl run mywebserver --image=my_webserver:0.3 --image-pull-policy=Never --restart=Never --port=8080
pod "mywebserver" created
$ kubectl expose pod mywebserver --type=NodePort
service "mywebserver" exposed
```

Visit you little Pod a few times:

```
$ curl $(minikube service mywebserver --url)
```

And now run the following command:

```
$ kubectl logs mywebserver
```

Nothing. Could it be that this Pod doesn't log any access requests? Let try it locally by just running the code and checking what happens when we visit it. You'll need two terminals for this. On the first one, start the app simply with python3 ./my_webserver.py. On the second, run this:

```
echo "GET / HTTP/1.0" | nc localhost 8080
```

Look there, the script does create log lines! Why aren't they showing up when we request them via kubectl logs? Let's do some investigating. First, stop the running my_webserver.py on your local machine (you can just press Ctrl+C in that terminal) and restart it with the following command:

```
$ python3 ./my_webserver.py 2>/dev/null
```

Visit it again and you'll see that you no longer get any lines. In other words, the output is sent to stderr instead of stdout. That shouldn't matter, though, as Docker provides access to both streams. If you want to be entirely sure the output is indeed sent to stderr, you can restart the script as follows:

```
(PYTHONUNBUFFERED=1 python3 ./my_webserver.py 3>&1 1>&2 2>&3) | sed -e 's/.*/^[[1;31m&^[[m/'
```

Where you replace both instances of ^[with the actual key combination of Ctrl+v Esc. And all stderr output is now colored! Okay, so that's just a plaything.

The PYTHONUNBUFFERED variable is important here, as Python by defaults buffered it's output. Or rather, it's Linux' <stdio.h> that does buffering when streams do not correspond to terminals, which in this case they don't (as we're piping to a another process). This would cause it to delay sending the output to sed until the buffered was filled or a specific buffer flush was called. Might that be the solution for our Pod? Let's try it, modify the Dockerfile so it looks like this:

```
FROM python:alpine3.6
ENV PYTHONUNBUFFERED=1
WORKDIR /usr/src/app
COPY my_webserver.py ./
CMD ["python", "./my_webserver.py"]
```

Rebuild our image and try it (just the commands here):

```
docker build -t my_webserver:0.4 .
kubectl run mywebserver --image=my_webserver:0.4 --image-pull-policy=Never --restart=Never --port=8080
curl $(minikube service mywebserver --url)
kubectl logs mywebserver
```

Cool, we have output. Let's recap.

We need to make sure with Python (and probably other languages as well, as this is mostly a Linux thing) that output is send to stdout or stderr unbuffered. At that point, it's captured by Docker and available with kubectl logs.

But I don't like how log lines that are not errors are sent to stderr, they should be sent to stdout instead. Let's change that in the code. Our next version will now look like this:

```python
import http.server
import sys
import threading
import signal

class MyWebpage(http.server.BaseHTTPRequestHandler):
    def do_GET(s):
        s.send_response(200)
        s.send_header('Content-Type', 'text/html')
        s.end_headers()
        s.wfile.write(b'''
<!DOCTYPE html>
<html>
  <head>
    <title>Hello!</title>
  </head>
  <body>
    <p>This is a demo page!</p>
  </body>
</html>''')

    def log_message(self, format, *args):
        sys.stdout.write("%s - - [%s] %s\n" %
            (self.address_string(),
             self.log_date_time_string(),
             format%args))
```

```
if __name__ == '__main__':
    def do_shutdown(signum, frame):
        threading.Thread(target = httpd.shutdown).start()
        sys.exit(0)


    signal.signal(signal.SIGTERM, do_shutdown)

    httpd = http.server.HTTPServer(('0.0.0.0', 8080), MyWebpage)
    httpd.serve_forever()
```

I simply override the log_message function with more or less the same function. You can see the original one here. As you can see, we simply copy the content from upstream and modify it a bit to use stdout instead. Let's build and run our new script and see if we get some output this time:

```
$ docker build -t my_webserver:0.5 .
Sending build context to Docker daemon  3.584kB
Step 1 : FROM python:alpine3.6
 ---> 1b1ac8f23f73
Step 2 : WORKDIR /usr/src/app
 ---> Using cache
 ---> 5ef4a439346c
Step 3 : COPY my_webserver.py ./
 ---> 60734f7c79ea
Removing intermediate container 9665c56c21c8
Step 4 : CMD python ./my_webserver.py
 ---> Running in b0fd71032822
```

```
    ---> 0ec32ff472aa
    Removing intermediate container b0fd71032822
    Successfully built 0ec32ff472aa
    $ kubectl delete pod mywebserver
    pod "mywebserver" deleted
    $ kubectl run mywebserver --image=my_webserver:0.5 --image-
    pull-policy=Never --restart=Never --port=8080
    pod "mywebserver" created
    $ curl $(minikube service mywebserver --url)
    ... (the output)
    $ kubectl logs mywebserver
```

JSON logging

Although Kubernetes does keep track of logs, once they are cleared from the disk on the node, their contents are gone. Therefore it is considered good practice to have a log aggregation mechanism in place for your Kubernetes cluster. The Elasticsearch stack (also known as EFK, Elasticsearch/Fluentd/Kibana) with fluentd seems pretty common and it is the one we prefer as well. This setup, like many others, prefers to receive log entries as JSON formatted strings. That allows the log aggregator to better organise the data, which in turn allows you to say something like "give me all log lines that are associated with this web application for all Pods that did not return a HTTP status 200 code". You can probably imagine how useful this will be when you have 100 replicas of a Pod running.

Let's modify the output of the application to emit JSON log entries. I'm not going to completely dissect the response, but leave that as an exercise for the reader. Change the code to the following:

```python
import http.server
import sys
import threading
import signal
import json

class MyWebpage(http.server.BaseHTTPRequestHandler):
    def do_GET(s):
        s.send_response(200)
        s.send_header('Content-Type', 'text/html')
        s.end_headers()
        s.wfile.write(b'''
<!DOCTYPE html>
<html>
  <head>
    <title>Hello!</title>
  </head>
  <body>
    <p>This is a demo page!</p>
  </body>
</html>''')

    def log_message(self, format, *args):
        log = {
          'my_webserver':
            {
              'client_ip': self.address_string(),
              'timestamp': self.log_date_time_string(),
              'message': format%args
```

```
        }
    }
    print(json.dumps(log))


if __name__ == '__main__':
    def do_shutdown(signum, frame):
        threading.Thread(target = httpd.shutdown).start()
        sys.exit(0)

signal.signal(signal.SIGTERM, do_shutdown)

httpd = http.server.HTTPServer(('0.0.0.0', 8080), MyWebpage)
httpd.serve_forever()
```

Now build and run it:

```
$ docker build -t my_webserver:0.6 .
Sending build context to Docker daemon  4.096kB
Step 1 : FROM python:alpine3.6
 ---> 1b1ac8f23f73
Step 2 : ENV PYTHONUNBUFFERED 1
 ---> Using cache
 ---> 6099cbb7db7c
Step 3 : WORKDIR /usr/src/app
 ---> Using cache
 ---> 0518dfef5e4f
Step 4 : COPY my_webserver.py ./
 ---> 6aa1b76fa2b3
```

```
Removing intermediate container 1f91cdabfe1b
Step 5 : CMD python ./my_webserver.py
 ---> Running in 5727d0a6d980
 ---> d3d78d4e4f45
Removing intermediate container 5727d0a6d980
Successfully built d3d78d4e4f45
$ kubectl delete pod mywebserver
pod "mywebserver" deleted
$ kubectl run mywebserver --image=my_webserver:0.6 --image-pull-policy=Never --restart=Never --port=8080
pod "mywebserver" created
```

We're already at version 0.6! How about that... Maybe we should fix the way we deploy this. But let's leave that for now and start with testing our output:

```
$ curl $(minikube service mywebserver --url)
<!DOCTYPE html>
<html>
  <head>
    <title>Hello!</title>
  </head>
  <body>
    <p>This is a demo page!</p>
  </body>
</html>
$ kubectl logs mywebserver
{"my_webserver": {"client_ip": "172.17.0.1", "timestamp": "09/Oct/2017 13:21:00", "message": "\"GET / HTTP/1.1\" 200 -"}}
```

Nice, it works. An important thing to note here is the fact that we use a nested namespace. This is important, as Elasticsearch forces you to have unique keys of unique datatypes. This is needed for proper indexing of those keys. So we consider it good practice to create a separate key group (not sure if there's a better name for them). The above example would give you the keys:

my_webserver.client_ip
my_webserver.timestamp
my_webserver.message

If we decide to have another app, called other_server, which stores an array in the message subkey, it will not cause problems, as that key would be other_server.message. This won't conflict with Elasticsearch's tender internals.

That said, the example above would be even better if we moved the timestamp to the top level, as that's the main key used by Elasticsearch to index the data and it should always be a timestamp in some form or another. Let's fix that:

```
        ...
        def log_message(self, format, *args):
            log = {
                'timestamp': self.log_date_time_string(),
                'my_webserver':
                {
                    'client_ip': self.address_string(),
```

```
            'message': format%args
        }
    }
    print(json.dumps(log))
...
```

Rebuild the app and run it and check the output:

```
$ docker build -t my_webserver:0.7 .
Sending build context to Docker daemon  3.584kB
Step 1 : FROM python:alpine3.6
 ---> 1b1ac8f23f73
Step 2 : ENV PYTHONUNBUFFERED 1
 ---> Using cache
 ---> 6099cbb7db7c
Step 3 : WORKDIR /usr/src/app
 ---> Using cache
 ---> 0518dfef5e4f
Step 4 : COPY my_webserver.py ./
 ---> fefa4c2a3da5
Removing intermediate container 62ec5724be8e
Step 5 : CMD python ./my_webserver.py
 ---> Running in a3b8c02cec53
 ---> 96e5f342196c
Removing intermediate container a3b8c02cec53
Successfully built 96e5f342196c
$ kubectl delete pod mywebserver
pod "mywebserver" deleted
$ kubectl run mywebserver --image=my_webserver:0.7 --image-
```

```
pull-policy=Never --restart=Never --port=8080
pod "mywebserver" created
$ curl $(minikube service mywebserver --url)
...
$ kubectl logs mywebserver
{"timestamp": "09/Oct/2017 20:13:05", "my_webserver":
{"client_ip": "172.17.0.1", "message": "\"GET / HTTP/1.1\" 200 -"}}
```

And to make the last line a little better readable (you'll need to install jq):

```
$ kubectl logs mywebserver | jq '.'
{
  "timestamp": "09/Oct/2017 20:13:05",
  "my_webserver": {
    "client_ip": "172.17.0.1",
    "message": "\"GET / HTTP/1.1\" 200 -"
  }
}
```

That seems legit! Now that we have this, let's move on to the other part of gathering information about a running application: metrics.

Prometheus metrics

There really is just one solution for gathering metrics within Kubernetes, Prometheus. I know, there are other solutions, but they all seem kind of cobbled together. However, where Kubernetes is an offspring of Google's Borg, Prometheus is an offspring of Google's Borgmon. The two fit together quite easily that it's almost a shame not to use this strong coupling.

In Python, adding support for Prometheus is pretty easy. But it does entail installing an additional library. For that, we must create a requirements.txt file (you can name it whatever you like, but this filename seems to be the de-facto default in the Python world). Add to it the following content:

prometheus-client==0.0.20

There might be never versions at the time you read this, but let's make sure that for this tutorial, you're using the same version as I am.

The image that we use has support for pip, we only need to tell it in the Dockerfile to actually install the requirements as listed in the requirements.txt file. The Dockerfile ends up looking like this:

```
FROM python:alpine3.6
ENV PYTHONUNBUFFERED=1
WORKDIR /usr/src/app
COPY requirements.txt /requirements.txt
RUN pip3 install -r /requirements.txt
COPY my_webserver.py ./
CMD ["python", "./my_webserver.py"]
```

When you build the Docker image now, you'll notice the extra steps and a few seconds delay as the library is installed:

$ docker build -t my_webserver:0.8 .
Sending build context to Docker daemon 4.608kB
    Step 1 : FROM python:alpine3.6

---> 1b1ac8f23f73
Step 2 : ENV PYTHONUNBUFFERED 1
---> Using cache
---> 6099cbb7db7c
Step 3 : WORKDIR /usr/src/app
---> Using cache
---> 0518dfef5e4f
Step 4 : COPY requirements.txt /requirements.txt
---> 221e52f8825c
Removing intermediate container db1f42afad0e
Step 5 : RUN pip3 install -r /requirements.txt
---> Running in 32ed19f9740d
Collecting prometheus-client==0.0.20 (from -r /requirements.txt (line 1))
  Downloading prometheus_client-0.0.20.tar.gz
Building wheels for collected packages: prometheus-client
  Running setup.py bdist_wheel for prometheus-client: started
  Running setup.py bdist_wheel for prometheus-client: finished with status 'done'
  Stored in directory: /root/.cache/pip/wheels/b5/13/d7/d8fca1b2db87bd1f9e5894722d6b7db24d27f617d6f040498c
Successfully built prometheus-client
Installing collected packages: prometheus-client
Successfully installed prometheus-client-0.0.20
---> 02c86904ebd5
Removing intermediate container 32ed19f9740d
Step 6 : COPY my_webserver.py ./
---> 5951ccbe14a1

> *Removing intermediate container 27373d8add71*
> *Step 7 : CMD python ./my_webserver.py*
> *---> Running in 594c8fb528af*
> *---> e7bad8a8ee00*
> *Removing intermediate container 594c8fb528af*
> *Successfully built e7bad8a8ee00*

Awesome. Now let's use it in our code. For this example we're going to collect the time it takes for the webserver to respond to HTTP requests. For that we first need to actually import the library. Then we create a special object for keeping track of these numbers, which we'll call REQUEST_LATENCY. As you can see in the example, the object is a Histogram which we're calling my_webpage_request_latency_seconds. The second argument of the constructor acts as documentation.

Prometheus metrics are very simple; they just present a key with a value next to it. The value is always a floating point number. Using the Histogram object causes the app to create multiple metrics, that each show the number of requests that fall within a certain range (in this case latency in seconds). We'll look at the actual output in a bit as well and you'll see what I mean.

Sampling of metrics in Python is easy as well. You just add a decorator to the method you'd like to track. In our case, that's the do_GET method. That's it. That's all you need to do to start collecting metrics. Easy, right?

The last step is actually starting the listener. Prometheus tries to keep things dead simple, so all it does is create a listening HTTP service on a designated port. You can see it starting the server right before we start the actual webserver object that we created. I've assigned the random port number 9999 to it, but honestly, choose whatever you want (we'll actually get back to that in a later installment of this series!).

The entire application now looks like this:

```
import http.server
import sys
import threading
import signal
import json
import prometheus_client

REQUEST_LATENCY = prometheus_client.Histogram(
    'my_webpage_request_latency_seconds',
    'Time it took to process incoming HTTP requests, in seconds.')

class MyWebpage(http.server.BaseHTTPRequestHandler):
    @REQUEST_LATENCY.time()
    def do_GET(s):
        s.send_response(200)
        s.send_header('Content-Type', 'text/html')
        s.end_headers()
        s.wfile.write(b'''
<!DOCTYPE html>
<html>
  <head>
    <title>Hello!</title>
  </head>
```

```
    <body>
      <p>This is a demo page!</p>
    </body>
</html>''')

    def log_message(self, format, *args):
      log = {
        'timestamp': self.log_date_time_string(),
        'my_webserver':
          {
            'client_ip': self.address_string(),
            'message': format%args
          }
      }
      print(json.dumps(log))


if __name__ == '__main__':
  def do_shutdown(signum, frame):
    threading.Thread(target = httpd.shutdown).start()
    sys.exit(0)

  signal.signal(signal.SIGTERM, do_shutdown)

  prometheus_client.start_http_server(9999)
  httpd = http.server.HTTPServer(('0.0.0.0', 8080), MyWebpage)
  httpd.serve_forever()
```

Are you still with me? At some point I'm only going to show you the snippets I'm actually changing, as the application is becoming quite large. Can you see all the changes I've made? It's not a lot, but you get a huge amount of value out of this! Let's check it out, rebuild and redeploy:

$ docker build -t my_webserver:0.9 .
...
$ kubectl delete pod mywebserver
pod "mywebserver" deleted
$ kubectl run mywebserver --image=my_webserver:0.9 --image-pull-policy=Never --restart=Never --port=8080
pod "mywebserver" created

But how do we access those metrics? Remember the kubectl expose command we used in the very first installment of this series? We're going to use that one again to expose port 9999 as well!

$ kubectl expose pod mywebserver --port 9999 --type=NodePort --name=mywebserver-metrics
service "mywebserver-metrics" exposed

First we need to generate some statistics, try something like this:

> $ for x in 'seq 100'; do curl -s $(minikube service mywebserver --url) > /dev/null; done =

> This visits the webpage 100 times in a row. It's not a good test, but good enough for now. When it's done, we can check the metrics like so:

```
$ curl $(minikube service mywebserver-metrics --url)
# HELP process_virtual_memory_bytes Virtual memory size in bytes.
# TYPE process_virtual_memory_bytes gauge
process_virtual_memory_bytes 79060992.0
# HELP process_resident_memory_bytes Resident memory size in bytes.
# TYPE process_resident_memory_bytes gauge
process_resident_memory_bytes 17100800.0
# HELP process_start_time_seconds Start time of the process since unix epoch in seconds.
# TYPE process_start_time_seconds gauge
process_start_time_seconds 1507581925.57
# HELP process_cpu_seconds_total Total user and system CPU time spent in seconds.
# TYPE process_cpu_seconds_total counter
process_cpu_seconds_total 0.19
# HELP process_open_fds Number of open file descriptors.
# TYPE process_open_fds gauge
process_open_fds 7.0
# HELP process_max_fds Maximum number of open file descriptors.
# TYPE process_max_fds gauge
process_max_fds 65536.0
# HELP python_info Python platform information
# TYPE python_info gauge
python_info{implementation="CPython",major="3",minor="6",patchlevel="2",version="3.6.2"} 1.0
# HELP my_webpage_request_latency_seconds Time it took to
```

process incoming HTTP requests, in seconds.
 # TYPE my_webpage_request_latency_seconds histogram
my_webpage_request_latency_seconds_bucket{le="0.005"} 100.0
my_webpage_request_latency_seconds_bucket{le="0.01"} 100.0
my_webpage_request_latency_seconds_bucket{le="0.025"} 100.0
my_webpage_request_latency_seconds_bucket{le="0.05"} 100.0
my_webpage_request_latency_seconds_bucket{le="0.075"} 100.0
my_webpage_request_latency_seconds_bucket{le="0.1"} 100.0
my_webpage_request_latency_seconds_bucket{le="0.25"} 100.0
my_webpage_request_latency_seconds_bucket{le="0.5"} 100.0
my_webpage_request_latency_seconds_bucket{le="0.75"} 100.0
my_webpage_request_latency_seconds_bucket{le="1.0"} 100.0
my_webpage_request_latency_seconds_bucket{le="2.5"} 100.0
my_webpage_request_latency_seconds_bucket{le="5.0"} 100.0
my_webpage_request_latency_seconds_bucket{le="7.5"} 100.0
my_webpage_request_latency_seconds_bucket{le="10.0"} 100.0
my_webpage_request_latency_seconds_bucket{le="+Inf"} 100.0
my_webpage_request_latency_seconds_count 100.0
my_webpage_request_latency_seconds_sum 0.038089960002253065

Wow! That's a very long list of metrics created by adding just a few lines of code... I'm not going to explain all the lines (why would I need to, they are documented!), but just pointing out that you can see the Histogram at the bottom. That's the one we created. And it's not very interesting. All the requests were completed within 0.005 seconds. Nice, but boring.

So to illustrate what's happening here, I modified my own version of the code to present some random delays, just so you can how it would look in a more life-like situation:

```
# HELP my_webpage_request_latency_seconds Time it took to process incoming HTTP requests, in seconds.
    # TYPE my_webpage_request_latency_seconds histogram
    my_webpage_request_latency_seconds_bucket{le="0.005"} 48.0
    my_webpage_request_latency_seconds_bucket{le="0.01"} 48.0
    my_webpage_request_latency_seconds_bucket{le="0.025"} 48.0
    my_webpage_request_latency_seconds_bucket{le="0.05"} 48.0
    my_webpage_request_latency_seconds_bucket{le="0.075"} 48.0
    my_webpage_request_latency_seconds_bucket{le="0.1"} 48.0
    my_webpage_request_latency_seconds_bucket{le="0.25"} 49.0
    my_webpage_request_latency_seconds_bucket{le="0.5"} 49.0
    my_webpage_request_latency_seconds_bucket{le="0.75"} 52.0
    my_webpage_request_latency_seconds_bucket{le="1.0"} 54.0
    my_webpage_request_latency_seconds_bucket{le="2.5"} 67.0
    my_webpage_request_latency_seconds_bucket{le="5.0"} 89.0
    my_webpage_request_latency_seconds_bucket{le="7.5"} 98.0
    my_webpage_request_latency_seconds_bucket{le="10.0"} 99.0
    my_webpage_request_latency_seconds_bucket{le="+Inf"} 100.0
    my_webpage_request_latency_seconds_count 100.0
    my_webpage_request_latency_seconds_sum 178.68813334600782
```

As you can see, the Histogram shows nicely that 54 out of the 100 requests were performed in one second or less. 89 out of 100 completed within 5 seconds. Sadly, although Kubernetes and Prometheus work nicely together out of the box, actually setting up Prometheus to scrape our little application is a bit more work than what I want to cover in these series. So I'm going to leave that as an exercise for the reader! But if you'd like a sidebar-like post explaining it, let me know (details below) and I'll consider it.

WHAT IS THE DIFFERENCE BETWEEN KUBERNETES AND DOCKER?

From a distance, Docker and Kubernetes can appear to be similar technologies; they both help you run applications within linux containers. If you look a little closer, you'll find that the technologies operate at different layers of the stack, and can even be used together.

Understanding both Docker and Kubernetes is essential if you want to build and run a modern cloud infrastructure. Let's take a look to see how they both fit into the world of linux containers, and how you can use them when architecting your own applications.

Containers - A Quick Intro

At their core, containers are a way of packaging software. What makes them special is that when you run a container, you know exactly how it will run - it's predictable, repeatable and immutable. There are no unexpected errors when you move it to a new machine, or between environments. All of your application's code, libraries, and dependencies are packed together in the container as an immutable artifact. You can think of running a container like running a virtual machine, without the overhead of spinning up an entire operating system. For this reason, bundling your application in a container vs. a virtual machine will improve startup time significantly.

The above characteristics make containers an awesome tool and essential building block in modern cloud architecture. While the industry pushes towards building microservice architectures, containers help facilitate quick elasticity and separation of concerns. And while some may not yet be building microservices, traditional monoliths can be containerized and reap some of the aforementioned benefits.

This all sounds really nice, but how do you actually build a container?

Build and Deploy Containers with Docker

Docker helps you create and deploy software within containers. It's an open source collection of tools that help you "Build, Ship, and Run any App, Anywhere". Yes, it really is as magic as it sounds.

With Docker, you create a special file called a Dockerfile. Dockerfiles define a build process, which, when fed to the 'docker build' command, will produce an immutable docker image. You can think of this as a snapshot of your application, ready to be brought to life at any time. When you want to start it up, just use the 'docker run' command to run it anywhere the docker daemon is supported and running. It can be on your laptop, your production server in the cloud, or on a raspberry pi. Regardless of where your image is running, it will behave the same way.

Docker also provides a cloud-based repository called Docker Hub. You can think of it like GitHub for Docker Images. You can use Docker Hub to store and distribute the container images you build.

Manage Containers with Kubernetes

Once you've recovered from the excitement of spinning up your first few Docker containers, you'll realize that something is missing. If you want to run multiple containers across multiple machines - which you'll need to do if you're using microservices - there is still a lot of work left to do.

You need to start the right containers at the right time, figure out how they can talk to each other, handle storage considerations, and deal with failed containers or hardware. Doing all of this manually would be a nightmare. Luckily, that's where Kubernetes comes in.

Kubernetes is an open source container orchestration platform, allowing large numbers of containers to work together in harmony, reducing operational burden. It helps with things like:

- Running containers across many different machines
- Scaling up or down by adding or removing containers when demand changes
- Keeping storage consistent with multiple instances of an application
- Distributing load between the containers
- Launching new containers on different machines if something fails

Wait, Doesn't Docker do Container Management?

Kubernetes isn't the only container management tool around. Docker also has its own native container management tool called Docker Swarm. It lets you deploy containers as Swarms that you can interact with as a single unit, with all the container management taken care of. To be clear, Kubernetes does not interact with Docker Swarm in any fashion, only the Docker engine itself.

Using Docker with Kubernetes

As previously mentioned, Docker and Kubernetes work at different levels. Under the hood, Kubernetes can integrate with the Docker engine to coordinate the scheduling and execution of Docker containers on Kubelets. The Docker engine itself is responsible for running the actual container image built by running 'docker build'. Higher level concepts such as service-discovery, loadbalancing and network policies are handled by Kubernetes as well.

When used together, both Docker and Kubernetes are great tools for developing a modern cloud architecture, but they are fundamentally different at their core. It is important to understand the high-level differences between the technologies when building your stack.

THE ADVANTAGES OF USING KUBERNETES AND DOCKER TOGETHER

You might be hearing a lot about Kubernetes and Docker—so much that you might be wondering which one is better.

Well, there is no "better," because these aren't equivalent things. Docker is like an airplane and Kubernetes is like an airport. You wouldn't ask "Which should I use to travel—airport versus airplane?" So it goes with Docker and Kubernetes. You need both.

In this ebook, we'll run through a deployment scenario, how containers and orchestrators can help, and how a developer would use them on a daily basis. You'll walk away from this post with an understanding of how all the pieces of the puzzle fit together.

Everything Starts with Your Local Environment

So let me start with a typical day in the life of someone who struggles through every deployment. Then I'll explain how these two technologies can help. For practical purposes, we'll talk about the fictional developer John Smith. John's a developer working for a startup, and he's responsible for deploying his code to a live environment.

He struggles every time a new version of the language, framework, or library comes out and he has to run an upgrade. The problem is when things aren't compatible with what he's installed. When something's not working, he just installs, uninstalls, updates, or removes until finally things get back up and running. The struggle becomes even bigger when he has to push a new change after doing all of that to another environment. It's kind of hard to remember all the steps when we're in a rush.

One solution could be for him to work with virtual machines (VMs). That way, he can isolate all dependencies and avoid affecting any existing apps and their dependencies

While that could work, it doesn't scale. Why? Because every time something changes, he has to take a new snapshot. And then he has to somehow organize all the different versions of those VM snapshots. He'll still need to deploy changes in code and any dependencies to other environments. Now, he can screw things up in other environments, too, and then fix it, and that's okay. But when we're talking about production, things get risky. He has to work with production-like environments to ease deployments and reduce risk. That's hard to do.

Even having automation in place, deployments might be too complex or painful. Maybe John even has to spend a whole weekend doing deployments and fixing all sorts of broken things.

We all wish deployments could be as boring as pushing a button. The good news is that that's where Docker and Kubernetes come into play.
Use Docker to Pack and Ship Your App

So, what is Docker anyway?

Docker is a company that provides a container platform. Containers are a way to pack and isolate a piece of software with everything that it needs to run. I mean "isolate" in the sense that containers can assign separate resources from the host where it's running. You might be thinking this sounds pretty similar to VMs, but the difference is that containers are more lightweight: they don't need another OS to make software run. Containers let you be more agile and build secure and portable apps, which lets you save some costs in infrastructure when done well.

I know that sounds like a textbook definition, so let's see how this is beneficial by following the day in the life of John.

Let's say John decides to start his containers journey. He learns that Docker containers work with base images as their foundation to run an app. A base image and all its dependencies are described in a file called "Dockerfile." A Dockerfile is where you define something like a recipe that you usually have in docs (or in your mind) for anyone who wants to run your app. He starts with the .NET Core app, and the Dockerfile looks like this. Take a look:

> FROM microsoft/aspnetcore-build:2.0 AS build-env
>
> WORKDIR /app
>
> # Copy csproj and restore as distinct layers
>
> COPY *.csproj ./

```
RUN dotnet restore

# Copy everything else and build

COPY . ./

RUN dotnet publish -c Release -o out

# Build runtime image

FROM microsoft/aspnetcore:2.0

WORKDIR /app

COPY --from=build-env /app/out .

ENTRYPOINT ["dotnet", "hello.dll"]
```

As you can see, it's as if you were programming. The only difference is that you're just defining all dependencies and declaring how to build and run the app.

John needs to put that file in the root of the source code and run the following command:

docker build -t dotnetapp .

This command will create an image with the compiled code and all of its dependencies to run. He'll only do the "build" once because the idea is to make the app portable to run anywhere. So when he wants to run the app, only Docker needs to be installed. He just needs to run the following command:

docker run -d -p 80:80 dotnetapp

This command will start running the app on port 80 of the host. It doesn't matter where he runs this command. As long as port 80 isn't in use, the app will work.

John is now ready to ship the app anywhere because he's packed it in a Docker container.

So why is this better? Well, John doesn't have to worry about forgetting what he installed on his local computer or on any other server. When the team grows, a new developer will rapidly start coding. When John's company hires an operations guy, the new hire will know what exactly what's included in the container. And if they want to do an upgrade of the framework or some dependency, they'll do it without worrying about affecting what's currently working.

Use Docker to pack and ship your app without worrying too much about whether the app will work somewhere else after you've tested it locally. If it works on your machine, it will work on others' machines.
Use Kubernetes to Deploy and Scale Your App

So, John now just needs to go to each of the servers where he wants to ship the app and start a container. Let's say that, in production, he has ten servers to support the traffic load. He has to run the previous command on all the servers. And if for some reason the container dies, he has to go to that server and run the command to start it again.

Wait. This doesn't sound like an improvement, right? It's not much different than spinning up VMs. When something goes down, he'll still need to manually go and start containers again. He could automate that task too, but he'll need to take into consideration things like health checks and available resources. So here's where Kubernetes comes into play.

Kubernetes, as their site says, "is an open-source system for automating deployment, scaling, and management of containerized applications." There are more of its type, but Kubernetes is the most popular one right now. Kubernetes does the container orchestration so you don't have to script those tasks. It's the next step after containerizing your application, and its how you'll run your containers at scale in production.

Kubernetes will help you to deploy the same way everywhere. Why? Because you just need to say, in a declarative language, how you'd like to run containers. You'll have a load balancer, a minimum amount of containers running, and the ability to scale up or down only when it's needed-things that you'd otherwise need to create and configure separately. You'll have everything you need to run at scale, and you'll have it all in the same place. But it's not just that. You can also have the ability now to have your own Kubernetes cluster running locally, thanks to Minikube. Or you can use Docker, because Docker now officially supports Kubernetes.

So, coming back to John. He can define how he wants to deploy an app called "dotnetapp" at scale.

Take a look at the "dotnetapp-deployment.yaml" file, where John defines how to do deployments in a Kubernetes cluster, including all its dependencies at a container level. In this case, besides launching the dotnetapp, it's also launching the database using a container. Here's how the file looks:

```
apiVersion: apps/v1beta1

kind: Deployment

metadata:

name: dotnetapp

spec:

replicas: 3

strategy:

rollingUpdate:

maxSurge: 1

maxUnavailable: 1
```

```yaml
    minReadySeconds: 5
    template:
        metadata:
            labels:
                app: dotnetapp
        spec:
            containers:
            - name: dotnetapp
              image: johndoe/dotnetapp:1.0
              ports:
              - containerPort: 80
              resources:
                  requests:
                      cpu: 250m
                  limits:
```

```
          cpu: 500m
        env:
        - name: DB_ENDPOINT
          value: "dotnetappdb"
---
apiVersion: v1
kind: Service
metadata:
  name: dotnetapp
spec:
  type: LoadBalancer
  ports:
  - port: 80
  selector:
    app: dotnetapp
```

John now just needs to run this command to deploy the app in any Kubernetes cluster, locally or in another cluster:

kubectl apply -f .\dotnetapp-deployment.yaml

This command will create everything that's needed, or it will just apply an update if there is one.

He can run the exact same command on this computer or any other environment, including production, and it will work the same way everywhere. But it's not just that. Kubernetes constantly checks the state of your deployment according to the yaml definition you use. So if a Docker container goes down, Kubernetes will spin up a new one automatically. John no longer has to go to each server where the container failed to start it up again; the orchestrator will take care of that for him. And there will be something monitoring the stake to make sure it's compliant-meaning it's running as expected-all the time.

That's how you could easily get to doing several deployments a day that take around five minutes.
You'll Deliver Quickly, Consistently, and Predictably

Now you know what Docker and Kubernetes are, and not just in concept. You also have a practical perspective. Both technologies use a declarative language to define how they will run and orchestrate an app.

You'll be able to deliver faster, but more importantly, you'll deliver in a consistent and predictable manner. Docker containers will help you to isolate and pack your software with all its dependencies. And Kubernetes will help you to deploy and orchestrate your containers. This lets you focus on developing new features and fixing bugs more rapidly. Then you'll notice, at some point, your deployments stop being a big ceremony.

KUBERNETES VS DOCKER SWARM

According to the Kubernetes website, "Kubernetes is an open-source system for automating deployment, scaling, and management of containerized applications." Kubernetes was built by Google based on their experience running containers in production using an internal cluster management system called Borg (sometimes referred to as Omega). The architecture for Kubernetes, which relies on this experience, is shown below:

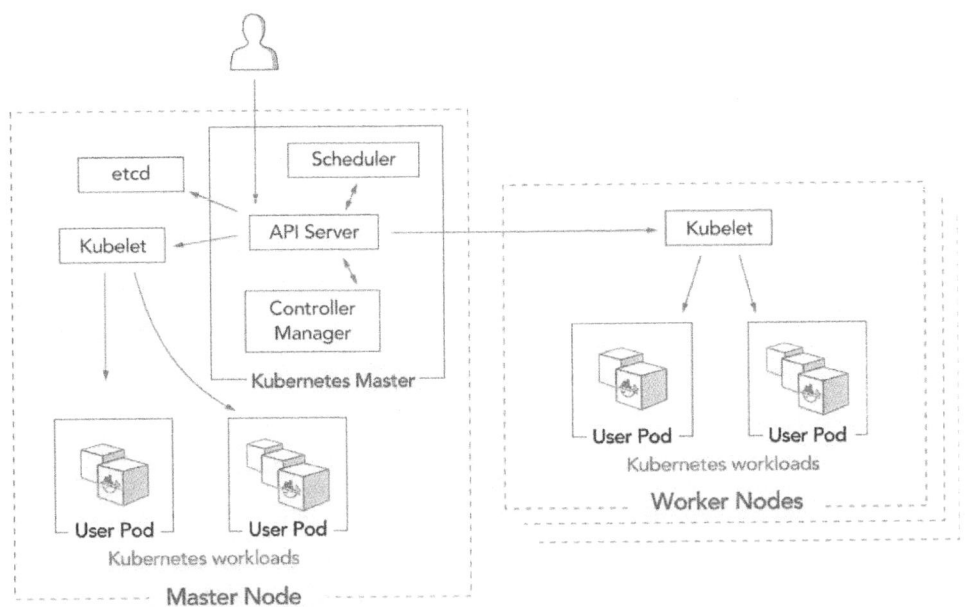

API Server: management hub for Kubernetes
Scheduler: places a workload on the appropriate Node
Controller Manager: scales workloads up/down
etcd: stores configuration data which can be accessed by API Server

Kubelet: Receives pod specifications from API Server, updates Nodes
Master Node: places workloads on Nodes
Worker Nodes: receives requests from Master Nodes and dispatches them
User Pod: a group of containers with shared resources

As you can see from the figure above, there are a number of components associated with a Kubernetes cluster. The aster node places container workloads in user pods on worker nodes or itself. The other components include:

- etcd: This component stores configuration data which can be accessed by the Kubernetes Master's API Server using simple HTTP or JSON API.
- API Server: This component is the management hub for the Kubernetes master node. It facilitates communication between the various components, thereby maintaining cluster health.
- Controller Manager: This component ensures that the cluster's desired state matches the current state by scaling workloads up and down.
- Scheduler: This component places the workload on the appropriate node – in this case all workloads will be placed locally on your host.
- Kubelet: This component receives pod specifications from the API Server and manages pods running in the host.

The following list provides some other common terms associated with Kubernetes:

- Pods: Kubernetes deploys and schedules containers in groups called pods. Containers in a pod run on the same node and share resources such as filesystems, kernel namespaces, and an IP address.
- Deployments: These building blocks can be used to create and manage a group of pods. Deployments can be used with a service

tier for scaling horizontally or ensuring availability.
- Services: Services are endpoints that can be addressed by name and can be connected to pods using label selectors. The service will automatically round-robin requests between pods. Kubernetes will set up a DNS server for the cluster that watches for new services and allows them to be addressed by name. Services are the "external face" of your container workloads.
- Labels: Labels are key-value pairs attached to objects and can be used to search and update multiple objects as a single set.

Overview of Docker Swarm

Docker Engine v1.12.0 and later allow developers to deploy containers in Swarm mode. A Swarm cluster consists of Docker Engine deployed on multiple nodes. Manager nodes perform orchestration and cluster management. Worker nodes receive and execute tasks from the manager nodes.

A service, which can be specified declaratively, consists of tasks that can be run on Swarm nodes. Services can be replicated to run on multiple nodes. In the replicated services model, ingress load balancing and internal DNS can be used to provide highly available service endpoints.

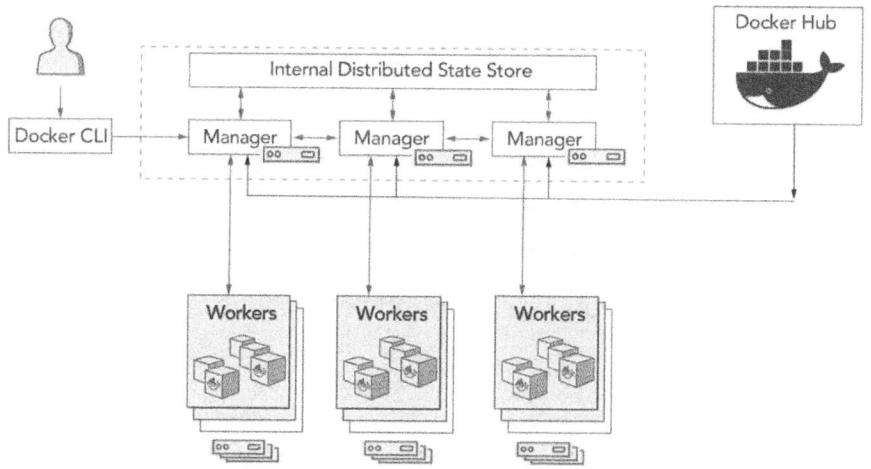

Manager: a node that dispatches tasks
Worker: a node that executes tasks provided by a Manager
Internal Distributed Store: used to maintain cluster state

Docker CLI: User interacts with the swarm using Docker CLI, for example "docker service"
Docker Hub: contains repositories for downloading and sharing container images

As can be seen from the figure above, the Docker Swarm architecture consists of managers and workers. The user can declaratively specify the desired state of various services to run in the Swarm cluster using YAML files. Here are some common terms associated with Docker Swarm:

- Node: A node is an instance of a Swarm. Nodes can be distributed on-premises or in public clouds.
- Swarm: a cluster of nodes (or Docker Engines). In Swarm mode, you orchestrate services, instead of running container commands.
- Manager Nodes: These nodes receive service definitions from the user, and dispatch work to worker nodes. Manager nodes can also perform the duties of worker nodes.
- Worker Nodes: These nodes collect and run tasks from manager nodes.
- Service: A service specifies the container image and the number of replicas. Here is an example of a service command which will be scheduled on 2 available nodes:

docker service create --replicas 2 --name mynginx nginx

Task: A task is an atomic unit of a Service scheduled on a worker node. In the example above, two tasks would be scheduled by a master node on two worker nodes (assuming they are not scheduled on the Master itself). The two tasks will run independently of each other.

DOCKER VS. KUBERNETES VS. APACHE MESOS: WHY WHAT YOU THINK YOU KNOW IS PROBABLY WRONG

There are countless discussions, and lots of social chatter comparing Docker, Kubernetes, and Mesos. If you listen to the partially-informed, you'd think that the three open source projects are in a fight-to-the death for container supremacy. You'd also believe that picking one over the other is almost a religious choice; with true believers espousing their faith and burning heretics who would dare to consider an alternative.

While all three technologies make it possible to use containers to deploy, manage, and scale applications, in reality they each solve for different things and are rooted in very different contexts. In fact, none of these three widely adopted toolchains is completely like the others.

Instead of comparing the overlapping features of these fast-evolving technologies, let's revisit each project's original mission, architectures, and how they can complement and interact with each other.

Let's start with Docker...

Docker Inc., today started as a Platform-as-a-Service startup named dotCloud. The dotCloud team found that managing dependencies and binaries across many applications and customers required significant effort. So they combined some of the capabilities of Linux cgroups and namespaces into a single and easy to use package so that applications can consistently run on any infrastructure. This package is the Docker image, which provides the following capabilities:

- Packages the application and the libraries in a single package (the Docker Image), so applications can consistently be deployed across many environments;
- Provides Git-like semantics, such as "docker push", "docker commit" to make it easy for application developers to quickly adopt the new technology and incorporate it in their existing workflows;
- Define Docker images as immutable layers, enabling immutable infrastructure. Committed changes are stored as an individual read-only layers, making it easy to re-use images and track changes. Layers also save disk space and network traffic by only transporting the updates instead of entire images;
- Run Docker containers by instantiating the immutable image with a writable layer that can temporarily store runtime changes, making it easy to deploy and scale multiple instances of the applications quickly.

Docker grew in popularity, and developers started to move from running containers on their laptops to running them in production. Additional tooling was needed to coordinate these containers across multiple machines, known as container orchestration. Interestingly, one of the first container orchestrators that supported Docker images (June 2014) was Marathon on Apache Mesos (which we'll describe in more detail below). That year, Solomon Hykes, founder and CTO of Docker, recommended Mesos as "the gold standard for production clusters". Soon after, many container orchestration technologies in addition to Marathon on Mesos emerged: Nomad, Kubernetes and, not surprisingly, Docker Swarm (now part of Docker Engine).

As Docker moved to commercialize the open source file format, the company also started introducing tools to complement the core Docker file format and runtime engine, including:

- Docker hub for public storage of Docker images;
- Docker registry for storing it on-premise;
- Docker cloud, a managed service for building and running containers;
- Docker datacenter as a commercial offering embodying many Docker technologies.

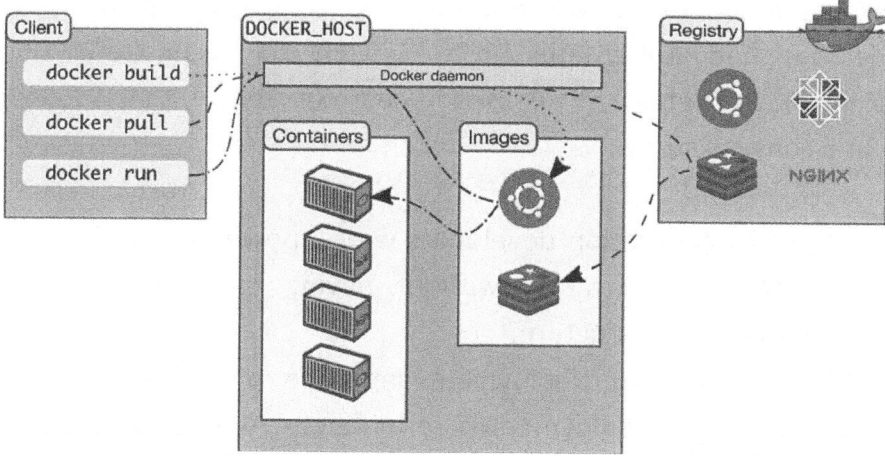

Docker's insight to encapsulate software and its dependencies in a single package have been a game changer for the software industry; the same way mp3's helped to reshape the music industry. The Docker file format became the industry standard, and leading container technology vendors (including Docker, Google, Pivotal, Mesosphere and many others) formed the Cloud Native Computing Foundation (CNCF) and Open Container Initiative (OCI). Today, CNCF and OCI aim to ensure interoperability and standardized interfaces across container technologies and ensure that any Docker container, built using any tools, can run on any runtime or infrastructure.

Enter Kubernetes

Google recognized the potential of the Docker image early on and sought to deliver container orchestration "as-a-service" on the Google Cloud Platform. Google had tremendous experience with containers (they introduced cgroups in Linux) but existing internal container and distributed computing tools like Borg were directly coupled to their infrastructure. So, instead of using any code from their existing systems, Google designed Kubernetes from scratch to orchestrate Docker containers. Kubernetes was released in February 2015 with the following goals and considerations:

- Empower application developers with a powerful tool for Docker container orchestration without having to interact with the underlying infrastructure;
- Provide standard deployment interface and primitives for a consistent app deployment experience and APIs across clouds;
- Build on a Modular API core that allows vendors to integrate systems around the core Kubernetes technology.

By March 2016, Google donated Kubernetes to CNCF, and remains today the lead contributor to the project (followed by Redhat, CoreOS and others).

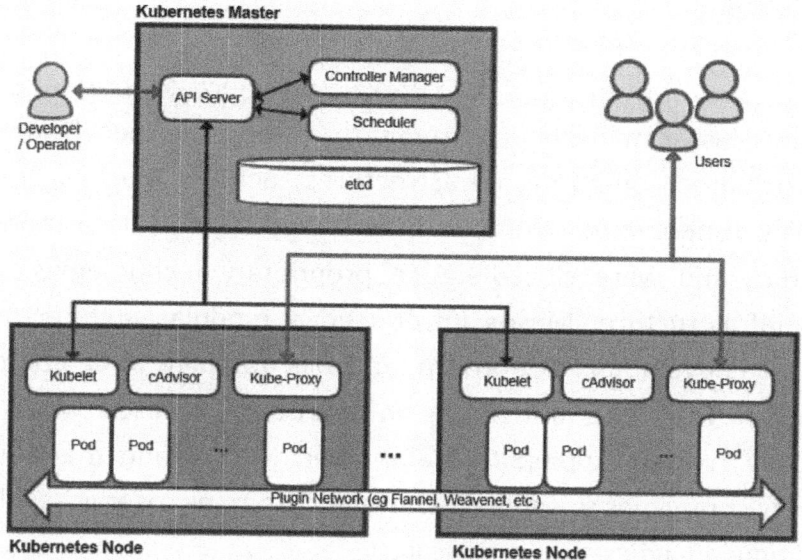

Kubernetes was very attractive for application developers, as it reduced their dependency on infrastructure and operations teams. Vendors also liked Kubernetes because it provided an easy way to embrace the container movement and provide a commercial solution to the operational challenges of running your own Kubernetes deployment (which remains a non-trivial exercise). Kubernetes is also attractive because it is open source under the CNCF, in contrast to Docker Swarm which, though open source, is tightly controlled by Docker, Inc.

Kubernetes' core strength is providing application developers powerful tools for orchestrating stateless Docker containers. While there are multiple initiatives to expand the scope of the project to more workloads (like analytics and stateful data services), these initiatives are still in very early phases and it remains to be seen how successful they may be.

Apache Mesos

Apache Mesos started as a UC Berkeley project to create a next-generation cluster manager, and apply the lessons learned from cloud-scale, distributed computing infrastructures such as Google's Borg and Facebook's Tupperware. While Borg and Tupperware had a monolithic architecture and were closed-source proprietary technologies tied to physical infrastructure, Mesos introduced a modular architecture, an open source development approach, and was designed to be completely independent from the underlying infrastructure. Mesos was quickly adopted by Twitter, Apple(Siri), Yelp, Uber, Netflix, and many leading technology companies to support everything from microservices, big data and real time analytics, to elastic scaling.

As a cluster manager, Mesos was architected to solve for a very different set of challenges:

- Abstract data center resources into a single pool to simplify resource allocation while providing a consistent application and operational experience across private or public clouds;
- Colocate diverse workloads on the same infrastructure such analytics, stateless microservices, distributed data services and traditional apps to improve utilization and reduce cost and footprint;
- Automate day-two operations for application-specific tasks such as deployment, self healing, scaling, and upgrades; providing a highly available fault tolerant infrastructure;
- Provide evergreen extensibility to run new application and technologies without modifying the cluster manager or any of the

existing applications built on top of it;
- Elastically scale the application and the underlying infrastructure from a handful, to tens, to tens of thousands of nodes.

Mesos has a unique ability to individually manage a diverse set of workloads — including traditional applications such as Java, stateless Docker microservices, batch jobs, real-time analytics, and stateful distributed data services. Mesos' broad workload coverage comes from its two-level architecture, which enables "application-aware" scheduling. Application-aware scheduling is accomplished by encapsulating the application-specific operational logic in a "Mesos framework" (analogous to a runbook in operations). Mesos Master, the resource manager, then offers these frameworks fractions of the underlying infrastructure while maintaining isolation. This approach allows each workload to have its own purpose-built application scheduler that understands its specific operational requirements for deployment, scaling and upgrade. Application schedulers are also independently developed, managed and updated, allowing Mesos to be highly extensible and support new workloads or add more operational capabilities over time.

Take, for example, how a team manages upgrades. Stateless application can benefit from a "blue/green" deployment approach; where another complete version of the app is spun up while the old one is still live, and traffic switches to the new app when ready and the old app is destroyed. But upgrading a data workload like HDFS or Cassandra requires taking the nodes offline one at a time, preserving local data volumes to avoid data loss, performing the upgrade in-place with a specific sequence, and executing special checks and commands on each node type before and after the upgrade. Any of these steps are app or service specific, and may even be version specific. This makes it incredibly challenging to manage data services with a conventional container orchestration scheduler.

Mesos' ability to manage each workload the way it wants to be treated has led many companies to use Mesos as a single unified platform to run a combination of microservices and data services together. A common reference architecture for running data-intensive applications is the "SMACK stack".

A Moment of Clarity

Notice that we haven't said anything about container orchestration to describe Apache Mesos. So why do people automatically associate Mesos with container orchestration? Container orchestration is one example of a workload that can run on Mesos' modular architecture, and it's done using a specialized orchestration "framework" built on top of Mesos called Marathon. Marathon was originally developed to orchestrate app archives (like JARs, tarballs, ZIP files) in cgroup containers, and was one of the first container orchestrators to support Docker containers in 2014.

So when people compare Docker and Kubernetes to Mesos, they are actually comparing Kubernetes and Docker Swarm to Marathon running on Mesos.

Why does this matter? Because Mesos frankly doesn't care what's running on top of it. Mesos can elastically provide cluster services for Java application servers, Docker container orchestration, Jenkins CI Jobs, Apache Spark analytics, Apache Kafka streaming, and more on shared infrastructure. Mesos could even run Kubernetes or other container orchestrators, though a public integration is not yet available.

Another consideration for Mesos (and why it's attractive for many enterprise architects) is its maturity in running mission critical workloads. Mesos has been in large scale production (tens of thousands of servers) for more than 7 years, which is why it's known to be more production ready and reliable at scale than many other container-enabling technologies in the market.

What does this all mean?

In summary, all three technologies have something to do with Docker containers and give you access to container orchestration for application portability and scale. So how do you choose between them? It comes down to choosing the right tool for the job (and perhaps even different ones for different jobs). If you are an application developer looking for a modern way to build and package your application, or to accelerate microservices initiatives, the Docker container format and developer tooling is the best way to do so.

If you are a dev/devops team and want to build a system dedicated exclusively to Docker container orchestration, and are willing to get your hands dirty integrating your solution with the underlying infrastructure (or rely on public cloud infrastructure like Google Container Engine or Azure Container Service), Kubernetes is a good technology for you to consider.

If you want to build a reliable platform that runs multiple mission critical workloads including Docker containers, legacy applications (e.g., Java), and distributed data services (e.g., Spark, Kafka, Cassandra, Elastic), and want all of this portable across cloud providers and/or datacenters, then Mesos (or our own Mesos distribution, Mesosphere DC/OS) is the right fit for you.

Whatever you choose, you'll be embracing a set of tools that makes more efficient use of server resources, simplifies application portability, and increases developer agility. You really can't go wrong.

WHAT IS CLOUD-NATIVE?

The term "cloud-native" gets thrown around a lot, especially by cloud providers. Not only that, but it even has its own foundation: the Cloud Native Computing Foundation (CNCF), launched in 2015 by the Linux Foundation.

Cloud-native' defined

In general usage, "cloud-native" is an approach to building and running applications that exploits the advantages of the cloud computing delivery model. "Cloud-native" is about howapplications are created and deployed, not where. It implies that the apps live in the public cloud, as opposed to an on-premises datacenter.

The CNCF defines "cloud-native" a little more narrowly, to mean using open source software stack to be containerized, where each part of the app is packaged in its own container, dynamically orchestrated so each part is actively scheduled and managed to optimize resource utilization, and microservices-oriented to increase the overall agility and maintainability of applications.
[What is Docker? Linux containers explained. | Dig into the the red-hot open source framework in InfoWorld's beginner's guide to Docker. | Check out our Docker tutorials: Get started with Docker. • Get started with Docker swarm mode. • Get started with Docker Compose. • Get started with Docker volumes. • Get started with Docker networking.]

"A cloud native app is architected specifically to run in the elastic and distributed nature required by modern cloud computing platforms," says Mike Kavis, a managing director with consulting firm Deloitte. "These apps are loosely coupled, meaning the code is not hard-wired to any of the infrastructure components, so that the app can scale up and down on demand and embrace the concepts of immutable infrastructure. Typically, these architectures are built using microservices, but that is not a mandatory requirement."

For cloud-native applications, the big difference then is really how the application is built, delivered, and operated, says Andi Mann, chief technology advocate at Splunk, a cloud services provider. "Taking advantage of cloud services means using agile and scalable components like containers to deliver discrete and reusable features that integrate in well-described ways, even across technology boundaries like multicloud, which allows delivery teams to rapidly iterate using repeatable automation and orchestration."

Cloud-native app development typically includes devops, agile methodology, microservices, cloud platforms, containers like Kubernetes and Docker, and continuous delivery—in short, every new and modern method of application deployment.

Because of this, you really want to have a platform-as-a-service (PaaS) model. A PaaS is not required, but it makes things a lot easier. The vast majority of cloud customers start out with infrastructure-as-a-service (IaaS), which helps abstract their apps from the underlying hardware. But PaaS adds an extra layer to abstract the underlying OS, so you can focus entirely on the business logic of your app and not worry about making OS calls.

Differences between cloud-native and on-premises applications

Cloud-native application development requires a very different architecture than the traditional enterprise applications.
Languages

On-premises apps written to run on company servers tend to be written in traditional languages, like C/C++, C# or another Visual Studio language if deployed on a Windows Server platform, and enterprise Java. And if it's on a mainframe, it's likely in Cobol.

Cloud-native apps are more likely to be written in a web-centric language, which means HTML, CSS, Java, JavaScript, .Net, Go, Node.js, PHP, Python, and Ruby.
Updatability

Cloud-native apps are always current and up to date. Cloud-native apps are always available.

On-premises apps need updates and usually are delivered on a subscription basis by the vendor, and require downtime while the update is installed.

Elasticity

Cloud-native apps take advantage of the elasticity of the cloud by using increased resources during a use spike. If your cloud-based e-commerce app experiences a spike in use, you can have it set to use extra compute resources until the spike subsides and then turn off those resources. A cloud-native app can adjust to the increased resources and scale as needed.

An on-premises app can't scale dynamically.

Multitenancy

A cloud-native app has no problem working in a virtualized space and sharing resources with other apps.

Many on-premises apps either don't work well in a virtual environment or don't work at all and require a nonvirtualized space.

Connected resources

An on-premises app is fairly rigid in its connections to the network resources, such as networks, security, permissions, and storage. Many of these resources need to be hard-coded, and they break if anything is moved or changed.

"Network and storage are completely different in the cloud. When you hear the term 're-platforming,' that is typically the work to accommodate the changes in networking, storage, and even database technologies to allow the app to run in the cloud," says Deloitte's Kavis.
Down time

There is greater redundancy in the cloud than there is on-premises, so if a cloud provider suffers an outage, another region can pick up the slack.

On-premises apps might have failover ready, but there's a good chance that if the server goes down, the app goes down with it.

Automation

So much of the cloud is automated, and that includes app management. "The benefits of cloud-native delivery, especially speed and agility, significantly rely on a substrate of reliable, proven, and audited known-good processes that are executed repeatedly as needed by automation and orchestration tools rather than through manual intervention," says Splunk's Mann. Engineers should look to automate virtually anything they do more than once to enable repeatability, self-service, agility, scalability, and audit and control.

On-premises apps have to be managed manually.

Modular design

On-premises apps tend to be monolithic in design. They offload some work to libraries, to be sure, but in the end it's one big app with a whole lot of subroutines. Cloud-native apps are much more modular, with many functions broken down into microservices. This allows them to be shut off when not needed and for updates to be rolled out to that one module, rather than the whole app.
Statelessness

The loosely coupled nature of the cloud means apps are not tied to infrastructure, which means they are stateless. A cloud native app stores its state in a database or some other external entity so instances can come and go and the app can still track where in the unit of work the application is. "This is the essence of loosely coupled. Not being tied to infrastructure allows and app to run in a highly distributed manner and still maintain its state independent of the elastic nature of the underlying infrastructure," Kavis says.

Most on-premises apps are stateful, meaning they store the state of the app on the infrastructure the code runs on. The app can be broken when adding server resources because of this.

The challenges of cloud-native computing

One of the big mistakes customers make is trying to lift and shift their old on-premises apps to the cloud, Mann says. "Attempting to take existing applications—especially monolithic legacy applications—and move them onto a cloud infrastructure will not take advantage of essential cloud-native features."

Instead, you should look to do new things in new ways, either by putting new cloud-native applications into new cloud infrastructure or by breaking up existing monoliths to refactor them using cloud-native principles from the ground up.

You also need to dispense with your old developer methods. The waterfall model certainly won't do, and even agile development might not be enough. So, you must adopt new cloud-native approaches like minimum viable product (MVP) development, multivariate testing, rapid iteration, and working closely across organizational boundaries in a devops model.

There are many aspects to being cloud-native, including infrastructure services, automation/orchestration, virtualization and containerization, microservices architecture, and observability. All of these mean a new way of doing things, which means breaking old habits as you learn the new ways. So do it at a measured pace.

MICROSERVICES VERSUS APIS

What Is an API?

First, let's define what an API is. According to Wikipedia, an API (application programming interface) is:

- a set of subroutine definitions, communication protocols, and tools for building software. In general terms, it is a set of clearly defined methods of communication between various components.

An easy way to think about an API is to think of it as a contract of actions you can request for a particular service. APIs are in use today in a multitude of web applications, such as social media, banking software, and much more. The standardized contract allows for external applications to interface with another.

For instance, let's say you're building an application that's going to integrate with Facebook. You would be able to use the Facebook Graph API to access data inside Facebook, such as users, post, comments, and more. The API simplifies the complexity of trying to use the data inside Facebook and provides an easy-to-use way for the developer to access that data.

Common API Actions

In today's world, APIs are usually developed using a RESTful style. These APIs will have a series of verbs associating with HTTP actions, like the following:

- GET (get a single item or a collection)
- POST (add an item to a collection)
- PUT (edit an item that already exists in a collection)
- DELETE (delete an item in a collection)

The advantage of this consistency through different applications is having a standard when performing various actions. The four different HTTP verbs above correlate with the common CRUD capabilities that many applications use today. When working with different APIs in one application, this makes for a recognizable way to understand the implications of the actions taken across different interfaces.

If you're interested in working with an interactive example, take a look at Reqres. Reqres provides mock data for interfacing with a RESTful API and the actions you can take when interacting with an API.

Okay, now that we have that covered, let's take a look at microservices. What Is a Microservice?

Microservice as:

a software development technique—a variant of the service-oriented architecture (SOA) architectural style that structures an application as a collection of loosely coupled services. In a microservices architecture, services are fine-grained and the protocols are lightweight.

But before we dig deeper into what microservices are and how they can be useful, let's take a quick look into the monolith. Understanding how microservices differ from monoliths will give you a better sense of the benefits of moving to a microservices architecture.

The Precursor to Microservices: Monoliths

In the early days of software development (and continuing in many large enterprise environments today), there's the concept of a monolith. A monolith is a single application that holds a full collection of functionality, serving as one place to store everything. Architecturally, it looks like this:

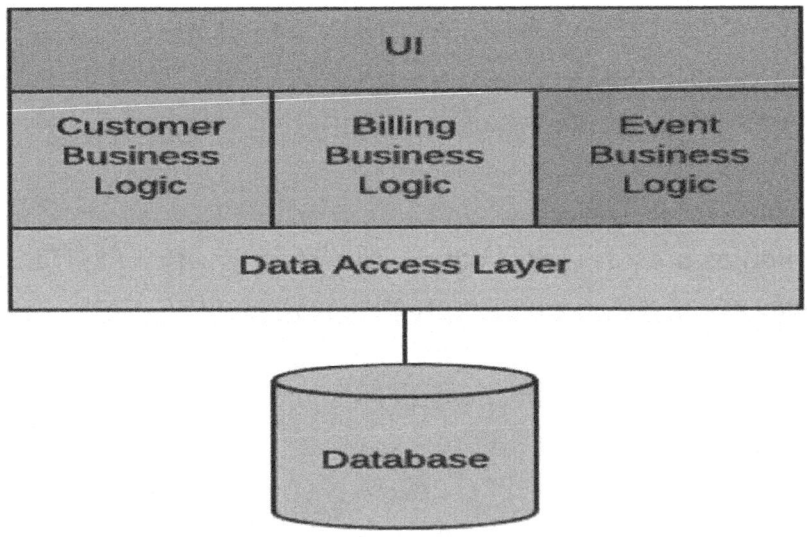

All of the components of the application reside in one area, including the UI layer, the business logic layer, and the data access layer. Building applications in a monolith is an easy and natural process, and most projects start this way. But adding functionality to the codebase causes an increase in both the size and complexity of the monolith, and allowing a monolith to grow large comes with disadvantages over time. Some of these include:

- Risk of falling into the big ball of mud anti-pattern, not having any rhyme or reason in their architecture and difficult to understand from a high level.
- Restriction of the technology stack inside the monolith. Especially as the application grows, the ability to move to a different technology stack becomes more and more difficult, even when the technology proves to no longer be the best choice.
- Making changes to the codebase affects the entire application, no matter how small. For example, if just one of the business logic sections is receiving constant changes, this forces redeployment of the entire application, wasting time and increasing risk.

So what's the alternative to building a monolith? Taking the monolith and breaking it up into microservices.

Enter the Microservice

Let's take the monolith example from above and convert it to use microservices. In that case, the application architecture would change to look like this:

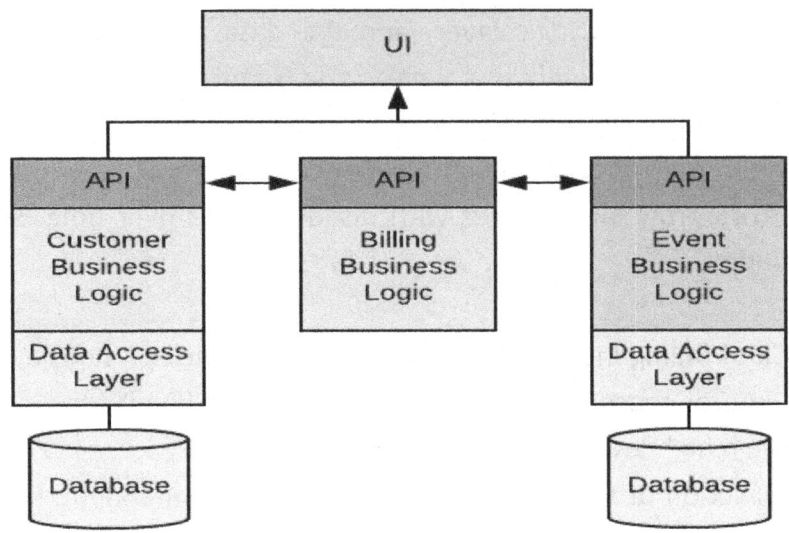

There are a few key takeaways from this re-architecture:

- The broken out sections of the business logic, each encompassing a microservice. Instead of having a single boundary for the entire application, the application is broken into pieces. The complexity of the application is reduced, as the different services have well-defined interactions with each other. For example, this allows for the capability to assign align teams to each individual service, encompassing responsibility in an abstracted piece.
- The UI layer from before only needs to interface with the customer and event microservices, removing a dependency for the billing microservice on the UI.
- The billing microservice does not need to store data, so it doesn't have a data access layer or a database. Instead, it interacts and processes data directly from both the customer and event microservices.

With this kind of architecture comes a whole host of advantages:

- It's easier to separate concerns. These boundaries between areas help with development (you only need to concern yourself with your microservice, not the entire application) and with understanding the architecture of the application.
- Unlike with a monolith, a microservice can use a different tech stack as needed. Considering rewriting everything in a new language? Just change one microservice to use the new tech stack, assess the benefits gained, and determine whether to proceed.
- Deployments of the application as a whole become more focused. Microservices give you the flexibility to deploy different services as needed.

In the example above, notice the API sitting alongside the other portions of the microservice? We'll get into that. It's finally time to talk about the differences between APIs and microservices.

The Difference Between APIs and Microservices

Here are the main differences between APIs and microservices:

- An API is a contract that provides guidance for a consumer to use the underlying service.
- A microservice is an architectural design that separates portions of a (usually monolithic) application into small, self-containing services.

By definition, this means an API is usually a portion of a microservice, allowing for interaction with the microservice itself. Another way to think about this is that the API serves as a contract for interactions within the microservice, presenting the options available for interacting with the microservice.

However, if we look at the microservices diagram above, we can see that each microservice is built slightly differently based on its needs. Here are a few examples of different functions a microservice can have:

- Providing CRUD operations for a particular entity type, such as a customer, event, etc. This service would hold the ability to persist data in a database.
- Providing a means to accept parameters and return results based on (potentially intense) computations. The billing microservice above may take information on an event or customer and return the billing information required, without needing to store data.

With the above example, you can probably see that a microservice is capable of being more than just an API for a system. An entire application can encompass a series of microservices that use their own APIs for communication with each other. In addition, each of these microservices can abstract its own functionality, drawing logical boundaries for responsibility in the application and separating concerns to make for a more maintainable codebase.

Conclusion

Hopefully now you have a better understanding of what both APIs and microservices are. Code maintainability and quality are both key parts of a successful IT strategy. Microservices help you stay true to them. They keep your teams agile and help you meet customer demands by producing high-quality, maintainable code.

Are you working in a monolith codebase? Think about taking a portion of that monolith and moving it into a microservice of its own. Once you do that, you should be able to see the benefits of using microservices. In fact, you might even decide to convert the entire thing.

WHAT IS MICROSERVICES?

Microservice architecture, or simply microservices, is a distinctive method of developing software systems that tries to focus on building single-function modules with well-defined interfaces and operations. The trend has grown popular in recent years as Enterprises look to become more Agile and move towards a DevOps and continuous testing.

Microservices have many benefits for Agile and DevOps teams - as Martin Fowler points out, Netflix, eBay, Amazon, Twitter, PayPal, and other tech stars have all evolved from monolithic to microservices architecture. Unlike microservices, a monolith application is built as a single, autonomous unit. This make changes to the application slow as it affects the entire system. A modification made to a small section of code might require building and deploying an entirely new version of software. Scaling specific functions of an application, also means you have to scale the entire application.

Microservices solve these challenges of monolithic systems by being as modular as possible. In the simplest form, they help build an application as a suite of small services, each running in its own process and are independently deployable. These services may be written in different programming languages and may use different data storage techniques. While this results in the development of systems that are scalable and flexible, it needs a dynamic makeover. Microservices are often connecta via APIs, and can leverage many of the same tools and solutions that have grown in the RESTful and web service ecosystem. Testing these APIs can help validate the flow of data and information throughout your microservice deployment.

The Six Characteristics Of Microservices

1) Multiple Components

Software built as microservices can, by definition, be broken down into multiple component services. Why? So that each of these services can be deployed, tweaked, and then redeployed independently without compromising the integrity of an application. As a result, you might only need to change one or more distinct services instead of having to redeploy entire applications. But this approach does have its downsides, including expensive remote calls (instead of in-process calls), coarser-grained remote APIs, and increased complexity when redistributing responsibilities between components.

2) Built For Business

The microservices style is usually organized around business capabilities and priorities. Unlike a traditional monolithic development approach—where different teams each have a specific focus on, say, UIs, databases, technology layers, or server-side logic—microservice architecture utilizes cross-functional teams. The responsibilities of each team are to make specific products based on one or more individual services communicating via message bus. In microservices, a team owns the product for its lifetime, as in Amazon's oft-quoted maxim "You build it, you run it."

3) Simple Routing

Microservices act somewhat like the classical UNIX system: they receive requests, process them, and generate a response accordingly. This is opposite to how many other products such as ESBs (Enterprise Service Buses) work, where high-tech systems for message routing, choreography, and applying business rules are utilized. You could say that microservices have smart endpoints that process info and apply logic, and dumb pipes through which the info flows.

4) Decentralized

Since microservices involve a variety of technologies and platforms, old-school methods of centralized governance aren't optimal. Decentralized governance is favored by the microservices community because its developers strive to produce useful tools that can then be used by others to solve the same problems. Just like decentralized governance, microservice architecture also favors decentralized data management. Monolithic systems use a single logical database across different applications. In a microservice application, each service usually manages its unique database.

5) Failure Resistant

Like a well-rounded child, microservices are designed to cope with failure. Since several unique and diverse services are communicating together, it's quite possible that a service could fail, for one reason or another (e.g., when the supplier isn't available). In these instances, the client should allow its neighboring services to function while it bows out in as graceful a manner as possible. However, monitoring microservices can help prevent the risk of a failure. For obvious reasons, this requirement adds more complexity to microservices as compared to monolithic systems architecture.

6) Evolutionary

Microservices architecture is an evolutionary design and, again, is ideal for evolutionary systems where you can't fully anticipate the types of devices that may one day be accessing your application.. Many applications start based on monolithic architecture, but as several unforeseen requirements surfaced, can be slowly revamped to microservices that interact over an older monolithic architecture through APIs.

Examples of Microservices

Netflix has a widespread architecture that has evolved from monolithic to SOA. It receives more than one billion calls every day, from more than 800 different types of devices, to its streaming-video API. Each API call then prompts around five additional calls to the backend service.

Amazon has also migrated to microservices. They get countless calls from a variety of applications—including applications that manage the web service API as well as the website itself—which would have been simply impossible for their old, two-tiered architecture to handle.

The auction site eBay is yet another example that has gone through the same transition. Their core application comprises several autonomous applications, with each one executing the business logic for different function areas.

Microservice Pros and Cons

Microservices are not a silver bullet, and by implementing them you will expose communication, teamwork, and other problems that may have been previously implicit but are now forced out into the open. But API Gateways in Microservices can greatly reduce build and qa time and effort.

One common issue involves sharing schema/validation logic across services. What A requires in order to consider some data valid doesn't always apply to B, if B has different needs. The best recommendation is to apply versioning and distribute schema in shared libraries. Changes to libraries then become discussions between teams. Also, with strong versioning comes dependencies, which can cause more overhead. The best practice to overcome this is planning around backwards compatibility, and accepting regression tests from external services/teams. These prompt you to have a conversation before you disrupt someone else's business process, not after.

As with anything else, whether or not microservice architecture is right for you depends on your requirements, because they all have their pros and cons. Here's a quick rundown of some of the good and bad:

Pros

- Microservice architecture gives developers the freedom to independently develop and deploy services
- A microservice can be developed by a fairly small team
- Code for different services can be written in different languages (though many practitioners discourage it)
- Easy integration and automatic deployment (using open-source continuous integration tools such as Jenkins, Hudson, etc.)
- Easy to understand and modify for developers, thus can help a new team member become productive quickly
- The developers can make use of the latest technologies
- The code is organized around business capabilities
- Starts the web container more quickly, so the deployment is also faster
- When change is required in a certain part of the application, only the related service can be modified and redeployed—no need to modify and redeploy the entire application
- Better fault isolation: if one microservice fails, the other will continue to work (although one problematic area of a monolith application can jeopardize the entire system)
- Easy to scale and integrate with third-party services
- No long-term commitment to technology stack

Cons

- Due to distributed deployment, testing can become complicated and tedious
- Increasing number of services can result in information barriers

- The architecture brings additional complexity as the developers have to mitigate fault tolerance, network latency, and deal with a variety of message formats as well as load balancing
- Being a distributed system, it can result in duplication of effort
- When number of services increases, integration and managing whole products can become complicated
- In addition to several complexities of monolithic architecture, the developers have to deal with the additional complexity of a distributed system
- Developers have to put additional effort into implementing the mechanism of communication between the services
- Handling use cases that span more than one service without using distributed transactions is not only tough but also requires communication and cooperation between different teams

How Microservice Architecture Works

1) Monoliths and Conway's Law

To begin with, let's explore Conway's Law, which states: "Organizations which design systems…are constrained to produce designs which are copies of the communication structures of these organizations."

Imagine Company X with two teams: Support and Accounting. Instinctively, we separate out the high risk activities; it's only difficult deciding responsibilities like customer refunds. Consider how we might answer questions like "Does the Accounting team have enough people to process both customer refunds and credits?" or "Wouldn't it be a better outcome to have our Support people be able to apply credits and deal with frustrated customers?" The answers get resolved by Company X's new policy: Support can apply a credit, but Accounting has to process a refund to return money to a customer. The roles and responsibilities in this interconnected system have been successfully split, while gaining customer satisfaction and minimizing risks.

Likewise, at the beginning of designing any software application, companies typically assemble a team and create a project. Over time, the team grows, and multiple projects on the same codebase are completed. More often than not, this leads to competing projects: two people will find it difficult to work at cross purposes in the same area of code without introducing tradeoffs. And adding more people to the equation only makes the problem worse. As Fred Brooks puts it, nine women can't make a baby in one month.

Moreover, in Company X or in any dev team, priorities frequently shift, resulting in management and communication issues. Last month's highest priority item may have caused our team to push hard to ship code, but now a user is reporting an issue, and we no longer have time to resolve it because of this month's priority. This is the most compelling reason to adopt SOA, including the microservices variety. Service-oriented approaches recognize the frictions involved between change management, domain knowledge, and business priorities, allowing dev teams to explicitly separate and address them. Of course, this in itself is a tradeoff—it requires coordination—but it allows you to centralize friction and introduce efficiency, as opposed to suffering from a large number of small inefficiencies.

Most importantly, smartly implementing an SOA or microservice architecture forces you to apply the Interface Separation Principle. Due to the connected nature of mature systems, when isolating issues of concern, the typical approach is to find a seam or communication point and then draw a dotted line between two halves of the system. Without careful thought, however, this can lead to accidentally creating two smaller but growing monoliths, now connected with some kind of bridge. The consequence of this can be marooning important code on the wrong side of a barrier: Team A doesn't bother to look after it, while Team B needs it, so they reinvent it.

2) Microservices: Avoiding the Monoliths

We've named some problems that commonly emerge; now let's begin to look at some solutions.

How do you deploy relatively independent yet integrated services without spawning accidental monoliths? Well, suppose you have a large application, as in the sample from our Company X below, and are splitting up the codebase and teams to scale. Instead of finding an entire section of an application to split off, you can look for something on the edge of the application graph. You can tell which sections these are because nothing depends on them. In our example, the arrows pointing to Printer and Storage suggest they're two things that can be easily removed from our main application and abstracted away. Printing either a Job or Invoice is irrelevant; a Printer just wants printable data. Turning these—Printer and Storage—into external services avoids the monoliths problem alluded to before. It also makes sense as they are used multiple times, and there's little that can be reinvented. Use cases are well known from past experience, so you can avoid accidentally removing key functionality.

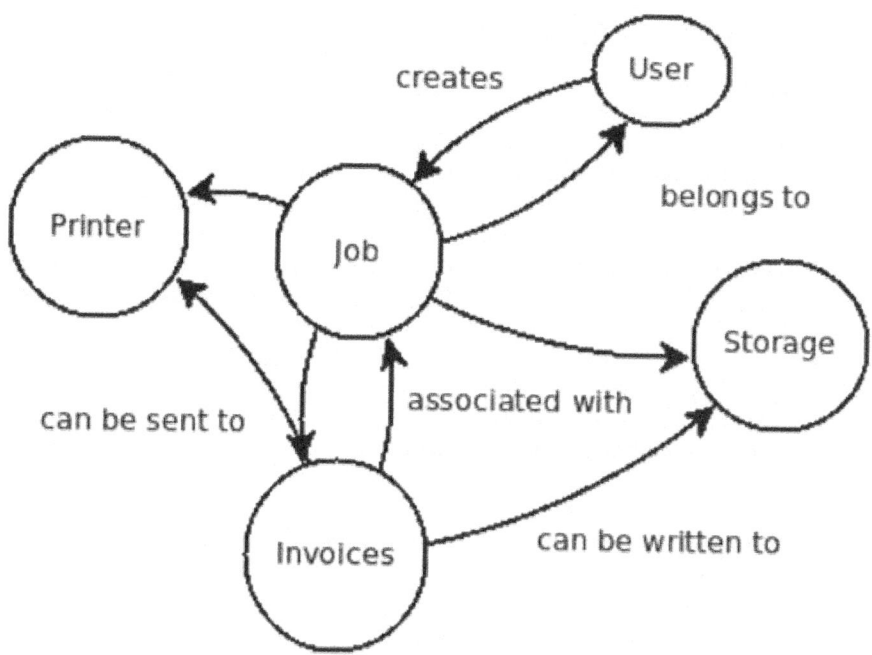

3) Service Objects and Identifying Data

So how do we go from monoliths to services? One way is through service objects. Without removing code from your application, you effectively just begin to structure it as though it were completely external. To do that, you'll first need to differentiate the actions that can be done and the data that is present as inputs and outputs of those actions. Consider the code below, with a notion of doing something useful and a status of that task.

A class to model a core transaction and execute it

```
class Job
    def initialize
```

```
    @status = 'Queued'
  end

  def do_useful_work
    ....
    @status = 'Finished'
  end

  def finished?
    return @status == 'Finished'
  end

  def ready?
    return @status == 'Queued'
  end
end
```

To prepare this to begin looking like a microservice, what's next?

```
# Service to do useful work and modify a status

class JobService
  def do_useful_work(job_status)
    ....

    job_status.finish!

    return job_status
  end
```

```ruby
  end

  # A model of our Job's status

  class JobStatus
    def initialize
      @status = 'Queued'
    end

    def finished?
      return @status == 'Finished'
    end

    def ready?
      return @status == 'Queued'
    end

    def finish!
      @status = 'Finished'
    end
  end
```

Now we've distinguished two distinct classes: one that models the data, and one that performs the operations. Importantly, our JobService class has little or no state—you can call the same actions over and over, changing only the data, and expect to get consistent results. If JobService somehow started taking place over a network, our otherwise monolithic application wouldn't care. Shifting these types of classes into a library, and substituting a network client for the previous implementation, would allow you to transform the existing code into a scalable external service.

This is Hexagonal Architecture, where the core of your application and the coordination is in the center, and the external components are orchestrated around it to achieve your goals.

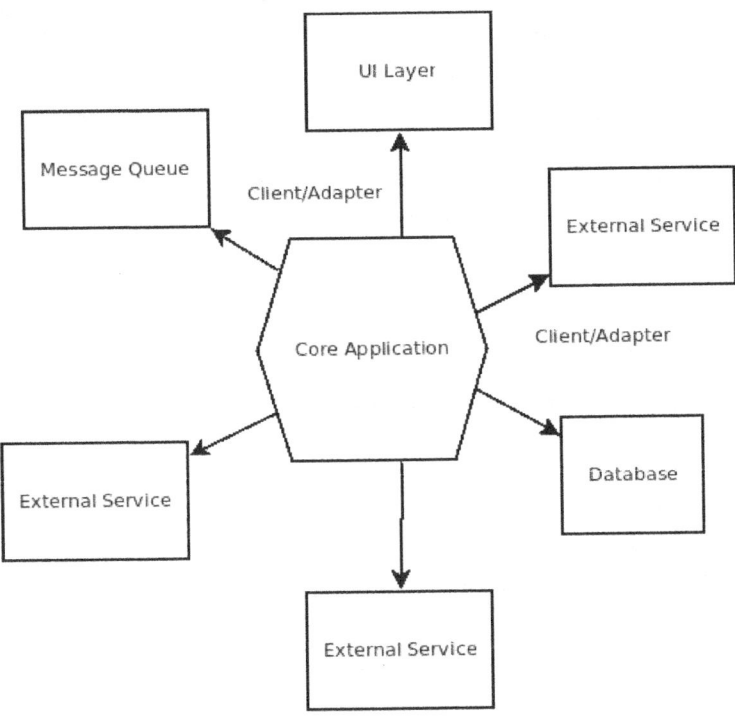

4) Coordination and Dumb Pipes

Now let's take a closer look at what makes something a microservice as opposed to a traditional SOA.

Perhaps the most important distinction is side effects. Microservices avoid them. To see why, let's look at an older approach: Unix pipes.

ls | wc -l

Above, two programs are chained together: the first lists all of the files in a directory, the second reads the number of lines in a stream of input. Imagine writing a comparable program, then having to modify it into the below:

ls | less

Composing small pieces of functionality relies on repeatable results, a standard mechanism for input and output, and an exit code for a program to indicate success or lack thereof. We know this works from observational evidence, and we also know that a Unix pipe is a "dumb" interface because it has no control statements. The pipe applies SRP by pushing data from A to B, and it's up to members of the pipeline to decide if the input is unacceptable.

Let's go back to Company X's Job and Invoice systems. Each controls a transaction and can be used together or separately: Invoices can be created for jobs, jobs can be created without an invoice, and invoices can be created without a job. Unlike Unix shell commands, the systems that own jobs and invoices have their own users working independently. But without falling back to a policy, it's impossible to enforce rules for either system globally.

Say we want to extract out the key operations that can be repeatedly executed—the services for sending an invoice, mutating a job status and mutating an invoice status. These are completely separate from the task of persisting data.

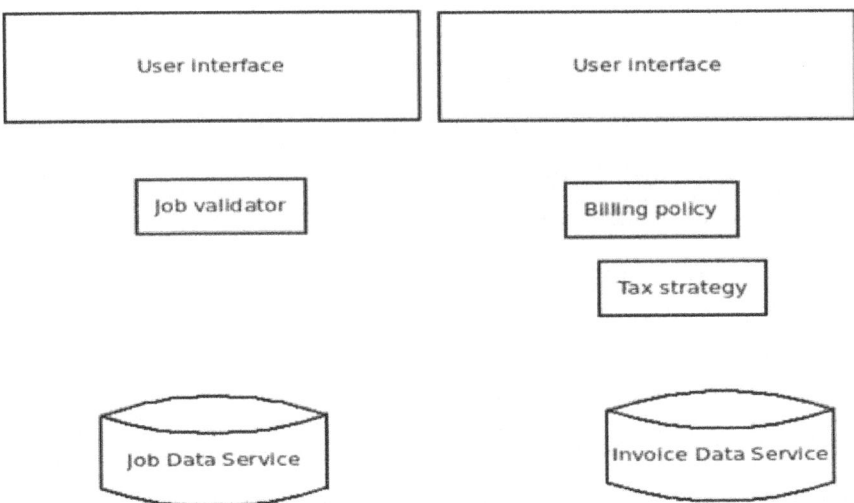

SOA vs. Microservices

"Wait a minute," some of you may be murmuring over your morning coffee, "isn't this just another name for SOA?" Service-Oriented Architecture (SOA) sprung up during the first few years of this century, and microservice architecture (abbreviated by some as MSA) bears a number of similarities. Traditional SOA, however, is a broader framework and can mean a wide variety of things. Some microservices advocates reject the SOA tag altogether, while others consider microservices to be simply an ideal, refined form of SOA. In any event, we think there are clear enough differences to justify a distinct "microservice" concept (at least as a special form of SOA, as we'll illustrate later).

The typical SOA model, for example, usually has more dependent ESBs, with microservices using faster messaging mechanisms. SOA also focuses on imperative programming, whereas microservices architecture focuses on a responsive-actor programming style. Moreover, SOA models tend to have an outsized relational database, while microservices frequently use NoSQL or micro-SQL databases (which can be connected to conventional databases). But the real difference has to do with the architecture methods used to arrive at an integrated set of services in the first place.

Since everything changes in the digital world, agile development techniques that can keep up with the demands of software evolution are invaluable. Most of the practices used in microservices architecture come from developers who have created software applications for large enterprise organizations, and who know that today's end users expect dynamic yet consistent experiences across a wide range of devices. Scalable, adaptable, modular, and quickly accessible cloud-based applications are in high demand. And this has led many developers to change their approach.

The Future of Microservice Architecture

Whether or not microservice architecture becomes the preferred style of developers in future, it's clearly a potent idea that offers serious benefits for designing and implementing enterprise applications. Many developers and organizations, without ever using the name or even labeling their practice as SOA, have been using an approach toward leveraging APIs that could be classified as microservices.

We've also seen a number of existing technologies try to address parts of the segmentation and communication problems that microservices aim to resolve. SOAP does well at describing the operations available on a given endpoint and where to discover it via WSDLs. UDDI is theoretically a good step toward advertising what a service can do and where it can be found. But these technologies have been compromised by a relatively complex implementation, and tend not to be adopted in newer projects. REST-based services face the same issues, and although you can use WSDLs with REST, it is not widely done.

Assuming discovery is a solved problem, sharing schema and meaning across unrelated applications still remains a difficult proposition for anything other than microservices and other SOA systems. Technologies such as RDFS, OWL, and RIF exist and are standardized, but are not commonly used. JSON-LD and Schema.org offer a glimpse of what an entire open web that shares definitions looks like, but these aren't yet adopted in large private enterprises.

The power of shared, standardized definitions are making inroads within government, though. Tim Berners Lee has been widely advocating Linked Data. The results are visible through in data.gov and data.gov.uk, and you can explore the large number of data sets available as well-described linked data here. If a large number of standardized definitions can be agreed upon, the next steps are most likely toward agents: small programs that orchestrate microservices from a large number of vendors to achieve certain goals. When you add the increasing complexity and communication requirements of SaaS apps, wearables, and the Internet of Things into the overall picture, it's clear that microservice architecture probably has a very bright future ahead.

Made in the USA
Middletown, DE
22 May 2019